MAPPING THE LINE

POETS ON TEACHING

Edited by

BRUCE GUERNSEY

Foreword by

TED KOOSER

Table of Contents

INTRODUCTION

by

Bruce Guernsey, Editor

When I was asked to edit *The Spoon River Poetry Review* in 2006, I had only recently retired from a thirty-six year teaching career. I'd grown weary of committee meetings and grading papers, but I had never tired of seeing a student's writing improve, whether it was an essay or a poem. All good writing is creative writing, I believe, and as a way to continue the privileged career I'd had, I started a feature in the magazine called "Poets on Teaching," now the subtitle of this book.

My plan was to ask the many fine poet/teachers I know across the country to contribute an essay per biannual issue. The requirements were simple: a practical assignment that had been class-tested to work, one that another poet/teacher could take directly to class and use. No jargon, no theory—just a straight-forward exercise of about a thousand words, and when I left the magazine, I had seven of such essays that I took along with me to start this collection of twenty that I have arranged in a semester-like fashion, beginning with the simpler exercises first. In fact, *Mapping the Line* could be the basis of a whole semester's work. There is also a subject index for specific assignments on such matters as metaphor and line breaks.

Ted Kooser's "Beyond the Classroom Walls" is the perfect "Foreword" here because of the tone it sets, asking us and our students to think beyond the poetry workshop to the real world outside it, one that is a little too busy to untangle a poem the way we all might do in a class. His argument makes sense, as do the exercises that follow his words.

Meant for the teacher and the student alike, *Mapping the Line: Poets on Teaching* is also meant for those who have never been in a poetry writing class but have, perhaps, been writing on their own or have been wanting to. There are some great hints on where to start herein because each of these contributors, whether a Pulitzer Prize winner or still struggling to get a book out, whether a professor in an MFA program or an itinerant adjunct, *all* of us had to start somewhere.

This collection is a good place to begin. And to continue.

Peace and grace.
—BG

FOREWORD

Beyond the Classroom Walls

by

Ted Kooser

U.S. Poet Laureate, 2004–2006

I've been thinking about the workshop tradition in creative writing education and wanted to pass along some thoughts that I hope may be helpful to both you and your students in your writing and teaching careers.

When a student takes a creative writing class, he or she is likely to have at least three fixed expectations: (1) that credit for passing the course will contribute to some goal, most often a degree; (2) that regular attendance and active participation in discussions will be rewarded with a good grade; (3) that the student will receive useful if not practical help with his or her writing. Workshops provide a useful service, and many accomplished writers have learned to improve their writing skills in workshops all over the country.

That's because a workshop encircles a poem or story with dedicated attention. The students enrolled are to be rewarded for being there, for paying close attention to a literary work, for devoting time to it. They are required to puzzle through its difficulties, to extend tolerance toward its every eccentricity, to try to be helpful and constructive. This makes for a remarkable experience, really, to have a whole roomful of people who are obliged to read whatever has been written, even if it's awful.

But that kind of attention is nothing like the indifference to fine writing ubiquitous in everyday life, and I know that some students enroll principally because they enjoy and value that kind of close, though otherworldly, attentiveness and toleration. Tuition pays for that attention, and the participants are paid for being there by getting a grade at the end of the semester. In short, the workshop environment is one in which attention has been purchased, and unless we as teachers acknowledge this fact, this artificial setting can lead a young writer to assume that the outer world is waiting on the edge of its chair to offer that depth of attention.

Sadly, the broader public does not look at literature in the way that our students and we so often do, sweating over texts because they are there. It is a delusion to assume that, say, a woman in some distant place, who is not taking a course but who happens upon a poem in a literary review, will devote a half hour trying to understand something that doesn't immediately communicate with her, to assume that she will fall upon it with great relish and spend a half hour picking over its obscurities in just the way a workshop participant might.

Sure, there are readers who will do that, who enjoy "solving" poems. I do not happen to be one of them. I also know that, when it comes to the breadth of the reading community, these people are few and far between. Ask yourself, for example, if when you are reading a magazine for pleasure just how much time you are willing to devote to writing that does not engage you, and engage you early. After all, you're not going to get three credit hours for spending your time in the way that students are, and you're not getting a grade. You're just trying to make the most of your precious time.

Nor are the preliminary readers and the editors of literary journals getting credit for paying close attention to our students' submissions, or our own, for that matter. It would take a rare editor, indeed, who would be eager and willing to spend a half hour studying a poem to try to make sense of it. He or she has a lot of manuscripts to look at, and some of the others in the in-basket may offer a lot more pleasure while reading them. And unlike the workshop, the writer isn't sitting right there, at the other side of the circle of chairs, to cry out, "But, here's what I meant...."

I ask you to remind your students that just because their peers in the class seem to be so interested in what they've written, are so willing to talk about it, to prod it this way and that, offering a comma here, a deletion there, doesn't mean that anybody else beyond the classroom walls will spend more than a minute glancing at it before moving on to something else. If we want to help our students find readers for their work, readers in the greater world, that is, we need to encourage them to write with that world in mind. Those folks in Hoboken are busy with their lives. They have bills to pay and children to raise and problems upon problems. They don't have a lot of time to spare, and because they don't, we need to foster writing that is willing to give them something, a poem that is indeed a gift, lines and stanzas that welcome those readers with open hands.

Intentionally obscure or obfuscatory writing may be accepted in creative writing workshops, where the attendees are rewarded for being there to ferret meaning from what may be nonsense, but it won't find a single reader among those hundreds of men and women breezing past the classroom door.

They Can Do It, Too

by

Baron Wormser

One of the marvels of poetry is how a good poem manages to be tactile and thoughtful, clear and mysterious, propulsive and unhurried—all at the same time. Teaching students to write such poems has never been easy since one wants to both inspire them and present them with some but not too much structure. To tell students to write a poem about spring and provide no further instructions is far too loose. To tell students to write a poem in Spenserian stanzas that deals with the consequences of the Versailles Peace Treaty is too tight. Students need a scaffold and some sense of direction; they don't need a map that marks every turn in the imaginative road. Poetry is discovery not rehearsal.

Over the years when it comes to getting students to write poems I have used John Haines' poem "The

Long Rain" as a sort of tutelary spirit because as a poem it is both a good teacher and a good inciter. Since it is such a short poem, I can dictate it to students, which I feel is the best way to get them to receive a poem—by writing it down word-by-word and comma-by-comma. I dictate it line by line and take plenty of time so that no student feels harassed. Not only does dictation get students to carefully attend to the poem, but it also engages their inherent curiosity—what is going to happen in the next line?

Here is Haines' poem:

The Long Rain

Rain falls
in the quiet woods.

Smoke hangs
above the evening fire,
fragrant with pitch.

Alone, deep
in a willow thicket
the olive thrush
is singing.

One of the beauties of this poem is how utterly straightforward it is. Whatever unhappy notions students may have about poetry—it is has to rhyme, have a secret meaning, make every last ounce of sense or make no sense whatsoever—Haines' poem tends to dispel. The first reaction to the poem is usually one of relieved delight as in "I can understand this." Yet as a poem "The Long Rain" uses many of the strategies I am trying to teach my students.

Thus my discussion of the poem begins with the use of the senses. The visual sense tends to be taken for granted in a poem but Haines' poem uses other senses to great effect. I ask students, "What other senses are used here?" They are quick to note the smells—pitch, smoke, and rain, for instance. They also are quick to note the sounds—bird song, rain, and the quiet woods. I emphasize that a poem wants to go beyond the visual sense; the other senses don't want to be left out. A good poem is not a tissue of abstractions. It lives in our senses by evoking the physical world.

I then talk about details with my students. When is Haines being specific? When is he using language that is explicit? Does he write "a bird is singing?" No, he writes "the olive thrush / is singing." He is carefully noting a very specific bird. He is even writing "the" rather than "a" and that is something we take into account: how

11

much emphasis is given to this particular bird. We go on to look at his adjective-noun combinations. He writes "willow thicket," "quiet woods," and "evening fire." He is deliberately giving further information that pulls the reader further into the world of the poem.

At the same time we notice that Haines is fine with simple language. He could have come up with other verbs than "falls" and "singing" but he didn't. I ask my students why they think that he preferred such unadorned language. This question (along with the others) keeps my students in the mode of evaluating each word choice and reflecting on how that word choice operates within the poem. In regard to Haines' basic verbs, students often observe that he doesn't want any word to call too much attention to itself. Indeed, he doesn't seem to want to call too much attention to the poem as a poem.

But we observe that the poem is carefully fashioned. We note the short lines, each one of which delivers some crucial aspect of the scene. We note the three stanzas. We note the use of the present tense—this is happening right now, almost simultaneously. We note how much space there is in the poem, how those white spaces between the stanzas give the poem a sort of rhythm. We note that it doesn't rhyme but there is plenty of attention to the sounds of the words, how, for instance "fire" and "fragrant" alliterate.

Then we write. My assignment can go anywhere because my dictates are simple: write three stanzas in short lines that don't rhyme about your evening meal or some historical event or your most recent athletic endeavor or driving around in a car or on and on and on. Use your senses beyond the visual sense. Use details and avoid abstractions. Evaluate each word choice—no clichés, no lazy language. Use the present tense. Try to use at least one metaphor or simile. I emphasize that these are spurs to good writing not Draconian strictures. These "rules" guide how writers write.

What I have found again and again is that students take right off from the Haines poem into their own imaginative worlds. The poem is a handy structure that opens doors for them. It grounds them but allows them to fly with their own wings. It empowers them. It shows them that poetry doesn't have to be fancy or arcane to be poetry. It shows them that they can do it, too.

Published Works Cited:

"The Long Rain," John Haines, *The Owl in the Mask of the Dreamer* (St. Paul MN: Graywolf Press), 1994

A Poem About Work

by

Kevin Stein

One of my favorite student assignments is the poem about work. Likely because I labored at a string of goofy jobs—carpenter's assistant, cable TV salesman, hotel night manager, cardboard factory line-worker, lumber yard crewman, Jewel Tea delivery driver –I've an affection for the variety and dignity of the American workplace. In daily conversation, it's always fruitful to get folks talking about their work lives, and the same holds for the medium of verse. As Hans-Georg Gadamer says, no one knows what will come up in a conversation.

Likewise, writers often let their guards down when they talk about the perils and pleasures of working, and often they do so in ways that surprise themselves the most, revealing much in the process.

15

Historically, work—physical, industrial, secretarial, managerial, whatever—has seldom been regarded as elevated poetic subject matter. It's as if most Americans have walled off our verse from an arena that consumes nearly a third of our lives. To say that work "consumes" us is no exaggeration: The physical and mental toll work exacts on our lives tests the spirit as well as the body.

How we overcome or merely endure that test measures our success in a capitalist culture where what one does for a living often determines one's rank or status. While we Americans don't abide by the trappings of monarchy or royalty, we easily establish each other's status by casually asking in a conversation, "What do you do for a living?" The answer quickly confers rank and privilege—or withdraws the same.

These are the sorts of "big" ideas that may emerge under the disguise of work-talk. Sometimes focusing on a job's particulars frees the poet's mind to see the larger social scaffolding propping up that job amid so much skittering and collapse. If the students (and you) are lucky, the poem becomes a pre-introduction to the spider web workaday world they are soon to enter.

Some Guidelines for a Poem about Work

1. Ask your students to use as subject a job they've held in the past, anything from a summer job to part time work or the labor of your lifetime. No doubt a student or two will claim never to have held a job, which says a lot in itself. No matter. Students can write about a volunteer position, too, if they've found in that role a sense of obligation and possibility. Even babysitting has its cultural context.

2. The trick here is to get writers to examine the position with a fresh eye, looking first from inside and then from outside its peculiar realm. If I fail at that, then my students produce mostly "I did this, I did that" laundry lists of their job duties. Ask what about this job strikes them (and potentially their readers) as memorable, revelatory, or simply bizarre? What about the job was initially foreign but then grew so familiar over time that they hardly noticed its exotic nature, say, the road crew job that closed every Friday evening with ritualistic burial of the week's road kills.

3. Nudge your poets to focus on how their role at work proffered an identity (perhaps one alien or new or even repulsive), one they readily accepted or thoroughly rejected. How did they change when they crossed the workday's threshold, both arriving

and departing the workplace? How does what they do define who they are, or define what others think they are? You needn't be an exotic pole dancer to understand how the imagery of a particular job inescapably paints its (self-) portrait of you.

4. To get started, I've found it helps for students to concentrate on the physical details of the job— sounds, smells, colors, etc. Suggest that they make a list of these sensory details, for instance, the scent of cut grass, the smell of bread fresh from Subway's oven, the stink of urinals blending antiseptics, ciga- rette butts, and beer-infused refuse.

The thorny part with all writers, young or old, is to prod them to translate this list of sensory details into metaphor and simile. Once students get the knack of it, they love the notion of call- ing the computer screen their pixilated love shack, or describing the restroom tile they mop as yellow as picnic mustard (or despair). With advanced stu- dents, I've had good fortune with short in-class exercises asking them to compose lists that merge particulars and abstractions such as this: grass clip- pings, Windex, and lust. The abstraction often star- tles students for its revelations about the nature of their labor.

5. Where students generally excel is in speaking the language of the place, the jargon, the dialect, the diction, and the slang of the workplace locale. If they defamiliarize themselves from the scene and its language, they hear it anew and recognize its palpably exotic (or merely quirky) qualities. The peculiar vernacular workers share with fellow workers infuses the poem with an idiosyncratic believability.

6. When I encounter students who balk at self-awareness, I try to get them there via the backdoor. I encourage them to turn the flashlight of their attention on a fellow worker—someone whose individual experience illuminates the larger experience of that job. That may be someone who has worked there many years, or someone so new to the job she is making the identical rookie mistakes your students suffered as newbies. There's always the boss as subject, or even customers as means of recreating a job's texture. For instance, one of my students, a liquor store clerk, wrote powerfully of serving bottled release to a daily parade of desperate graying drunks and underage college boys.

Whatever your students do, prod them to strive for authenticity, discovery, and surprise. Ask them to question the human nature of their job (and of work in general). Robert Frost's old saw applies here: That the poem can serve as vehicle for writers to find out what they didn't know they knew.

Sample Work Poems

For sample work poems by well-known authors, you can offer up James Wright's "Autumn Beings in Martins Ferry, Ohio," "Honey," "Willy Lyons," and "The Flying Eagles of Troop 62." Phillip Levine's "What Work Is," "Buying and Selling," and "Fear and Fame" serve as useful models as well.

Here's a work poem by a former student, Shannon Moore. Commonly, I break students into groups so they can read, discuss, and analyze how another student's work poem *works*. As this is frequently among student's first assignments, I've found it helpful for students to have in hand a glossary of poetic terms. I visit each student group as well and wheedle them toward examples of anaphora, enjambment, and the like. But the real star here is Shannon's intimate pondering of her work role and what it reveals of the inner self. I'm pleased to say that this poem about work won Bradley University's 2003 Academy of American Poets Prize.

A Confession

I worked for the E_____ cosmetics company
for three years, and a few months to my birthday.
I was a Diamond Star employee, friendly, well-versed
in the trade. In three years, I
fell in love
with many women.

I fell in love with women I worked with,
the pros, women who were there before
the new company bought the old company,
who spent their fluorescent, empty
department store afternoons swapping medical records
to soundtracked pop radio intercom,
gossiping in cigarette huddles all winter,
out behind the dumpsters.

I was in love with the women who prayed to be beautiful,
women who came to me for skincare redemption,
for a new doctrine of color,
who needed to know how to look younger, feel younger,
be younger. What mascara should they use to make
their eyes
look like mine, younger?

I was in love with the women who visited
the counter without their purse,
bribed, flirted, begged for free samples, free advice,
laughed musically, leaned in close
to reveal their worst sins:
I went to bed with my makeup on last night.
I was in love with the golden-aged customers,
with prominent names, coral lips,
their daughters and their daughters.
I gave them golden rules,
and they brought in their sweatered dogs and
eccentric sons for me to meet.

I was in love with the makeover women.
I craved the expression on their faces
the first time I reached out to touch them.
Rigid at first, unfamiliar with soft hands,
some smiled shyly, sighed, hummed breathed
the perfume from my wrist, and watched my face.
They fell asleep to the movement of my brush, then
flushed, laughed at themselves.

Face close to face, I fought incredible urges to kiss
women I touched, old or young,
women who came in with their fiancés,
stroller of young children, dozing hubby.

I was in love with the faces they made
in the mirror, when I was done
with my work.

I left my position at the cosmetics counter,
wilted in August, aglow with well wishes,
goodbye kisses, and something else
warm with guilt inside.
I had tasted what I desired too much,
and I knew all too well.

--Shannon Moore

Writing a Poem Using Scaffolding

By

Andrea Hollander

One of the most difficult truths for student writers to learn about creating poems is that the quality of syntax and the rhythm of language differ significantly from that of prose. Too often—far too often—these writers cannot easily understand (cannot hear or see) such differences. They often draft a poem by first creating a prose paragraph, then breaking it into (often arbitrary) lines, believing the resulting composition is a poem. With such students I often do a handful of exercises that focus on the line and the stanza, as well as on rhythm and rhyme. Besides these, one of the most successful exercises I have created is one that focuses singularly on syntax. In order to successfully understand the ways that good poems insist upon concision of language and rhythm is to use the successful poem of another poet as scaffolding.

Here is the exercise:

1. Choose an unfamiliar poem of *at least fourteen lines* from an anthology of contemporary poetry such as *The Autumn House Anthology of Contemporary American Poetry*, and type out the lines, leaving three spaces between lines. The exercise works best if you choose a poem containing concrete detail, proper punctuation, and left-hand justified lines.

2. Then, looking only at line one on the typed paper, *hand-write* a line of your own that corresponds in its syntax to the line of the "borrowed" poem but does *not* use any of its words (other than the occasional article or preposition). I'll demonstrate with the first five lines from Theodore Deppe's "The Paradise of Wings."

   Note that in the response a few liberties are taken; for example, in the response to line one, the word *sometimes* is added to the beginning of the line, a gesture not included by Deppe in his poem. The rest of that line, however, follows the basic syntactic format of the original: personal pronoun modifies generic name for a person followed by a verb (the respondent changed the tense from the original simple past) followed by an object pronoun. In line two, the respondent eliminated the article *the* and added an adjective to the noun of place.

> LINE 1: *My grandfather called it*
>
> RESPONSE: Sometimes my mother would tell me
>
> LINE 2: *the Paradise of Wings, a clearing*
>
> RESPONSE: Heaven, a blank field
>
> LINE 3: *hidden in blue hills where thousands*
>
> RESPONSE: frozen in a violet sky where so many
>
> LINE 4: *of geese gleaned stubbled corn*
>
> RESPONSE: clouds clung to stalks of sunshine
>
> LINE 5: *beside a tapered lake. His favorite walk —*
>
> RESPONSE: along the narrow road. My mother's window —

3. When you have completed the exercise, copy only *your* lines onto a new page:

> Sometimes my mother would tell me
> Heaven, a blank field
> frozen in a violet sky where so many
> clouds clung to stalks of sunshine
> along the narrow road. My mother's window —

4. Of course, your poem is not finished. Sometimes the syntax, which you modeled after the original poem, is awkward in yours. Usually the poem doesn't yet make sense. Your task now is to revise and shape the poem. You may want to alter the language, add or subtract lines, work with line- and stanza-length, inject or remove rhyme (external or internal), etc. Here is a revision of the five lines:

> Sometimes my mother would tell me
> Heaven was only a blank field
> frozen like the violet winter sky where so
>> many
> clouds cling like moths to narrow stalks of
>> iridescent light
> along the horizon. My mother's window –

5. The exercise above produces the first section of a two-sectioned poem. Now, following the impetus of what you've written and without "help" from the original poem by the other poet, create section two.

Note: Part 5 of this exercise is meant to help the poet to create a poem without scaffolding but still under its influence. Often this newly drafted second section is even more successful than the first section of the poem, in part perhaps because it is no longer hemmed in by the scaffolding's particular limitations but also because it has nevertheless been carried forth by the scaffolding's energy.

Final Note: Because the original poem is merely a guiding vessel and not a poem in a particular fixed form (as would be a sonnet or villanelle or other precisely formatted piece), the student who undertakes this exercise is not limited by such technicalities as meter or rhyme, even if the original poem utilizes them.

Instead, the student more or less "answers" the syntax of the original and plays with the components of language—nouns, verbs, adjectives, etc.—and with the possibilities of their contextual and syntactical place as the poet climbs the length of the original poem and matches its syntax to the new one.

Published Works Cited:

"The Paradise of Wings," Theodore Deppe, *The Wandered King: Poems* (Boston, MA: Alice James Books), 1996

Who's Writing This?

by

Cecilia Woloch

Who Am I?

I do not know who I am.

When I went looking for me, I found me.

But how would I know it was me?

So I did not know who I am.

I never met me.

— *Isaac Shaman, 1st grade, Hancock Park School*

The AWP *Writers Chronicle* recently ran an article by Reg Saner that articulated a few of my own suspicions about what happens to us when we write, where we "go" when we write, and how the act of writing changes us. Saner calls that place where the magic of language interacts with the lived experience of the self who's doing the writing an "ecotone." He posits that going to that place, that ecotone, gives each of us access to insights we can't reach any other way; and that the interaction that takes place there is transformative, brings into being another self, or an "enhanced self." And thus, "Your writing creates you as you create it." Willard Spiegelman says something similar in his essay on "The Pleasure of Writing": "You commit yourself in total concentration, but you also give yourself up in the process. In so doing, you find yourself, even though you are not sure who that person is." All of which my former student Isaac Shaman, at six years old, discovered for himself when I asked his first grade class to write about their names.

The self is a wonderfully slippery thing, and writing — especially writing poetry — allows us to slip around inside our sense of who we are and even, sometimes, to escape self-consciousness altogether. "Inspiration is the state in which you are so much yourself that you don't know who you are," the poet Phillip Levine has said. So how might a poet approach that state?

The Maps

by James Baker Hall
All those years he was married,
frequenting the map stores.
The eight quadrangles surrounding the house
in which he lived and worked, he saw them in
    relief:

he pinned them over his desk like messages,
    justified.
He spent long hours studying them. He fell in love

with maps. At night he would lie on the couch
with his hands, in the dark, memorizing
the mountains. He would lie
on the floor in his son's room,
in the moonlight, the maps
between them. His hands
loved the waters, an island
at a time. His voice loved
distances. At some point
he quit, I quit

calling myself he.
I fell in love without maps.
I carried everything I thought I needed
in the back of a truck or in a knapsack,
I spent night after night lost in the darkness,
huddled on a beach somewhere, or asleep
on a stranger's floor. It took years.
I had to go all the way
to the white undersides of the leaves
before I knew that my own veins were shaking,
in the dogs' ears, in the wind,

and it could occur to me, more often now,
that I need nothing. That I could, even yet,
quit calling myself anything.

The magic of this poem is apparent to everyone who hears it, as soon as they hear it. The poem turns on that moment of "he" becoming "I," when the poet shifts from talking about himself in third person, as if he were someone else, and begins to call himself "I," a moment that coincides in language with a profound shift in the speaker's life and sense of himself. Then the poem shifts again, at the end, when the speaker's sense of himself has expanded to the point that he needn't call himself anything.

The exercise I've devised, based on this poem, asks the poet to use a trick of language to create the distance necessary to meet herself or himself as a stranger in that place that writing makes. It's proven a fruitful exercise for mature as well as beginning writers and especially for those who feel, for whatever reason, reluctant to write in a "personal" way about their lives.

First, I ask each writer to think of a time in his or her life that feels like "a foreign country" now, one as long as several decades ago or, perhaps, a recent time of crisis or transition. I ask them to think about where they were living and what their habits were then—to remember the details and dreams of that time.

Next I ask them, "What was 'typical' of you then that isn't now: what kinds of things did you say, do, believe; how did you act, dress, love? What did you love? Who was that person?" I give them five or ten minutes to make some notes to themselves, then I say, "Think about when and/or how that changed, when and/or how *you* changed."

The rest of he instructions are simple: I tell each writer to begin writing about that era in his or her own life in third person, as if it were someone else's life, and to keep writing until that "he" or "she" changes to "I." The shift may occur on its own, "naturally," as it were, or at some point the writer may just decide to pivot the camera around and face his or her life again, from the other direction, head on.

If the writing exercise is being done in a class or group, I may simply, after fifteen minutes or so, give the signal for everyone to shift from third into first person. In any case, I suggest that they "pivot" in one line on a strong verb, as Hall does: "he quit, I quit," becoming, for example, "she laughed, I laughed," or "he swam, I swam." This point at which the language shifts may end up being in the middle of the poem, as it does in Hall's, or it may be near the end, or at the very end, as we see in the following poem by Jan Hanson.

Year One

In August, 1968, she was twenty-one years
    old.
Each week she pored though *The Betty Crocker*
New Dinner for Two Cookbook
and wrote down dinner menus for a week at a
    time
and posted them on the refrigerator.

He came home from work
one pot roast Tuesday and said,
"Oh, by the way, I had pot roast for lunch."

Every Saturday afternoon,
he lined up lawn equipment, tools, crates
in the driveway and swept, scrubbed,
while she cleaned the house inside,
vacuuming, dusting, stripping wax off lino-
    leum floors.

Afterwards, out for dinner with his friends
and their wives
who were not friends of hers,
he and his pals laughed about high school, the
    army,
life before marriage.

Sundays, he played golf. She went to church.

Mondays, he went to work as a department
    manager.
She went to school—
to become a teacher, to contribute maybe
to the household income
when not making curtains for the kitchen win-
    dows.

In January, the university informed her
she was disqualified.

Late that afternoon, she left the letter
by the weekly menu on the refrigerator
and drove around the neighborhood,
around and around
until she was sure he was home and had read it.

On a Thursday in February,
she went to the doctor for her headaches.
"Is everything ok at home?"
She said yes.
I said no.

    Jan's poem, I think, quietly achieves what Stanly
Kunitz called "converting life into legend": transform-
ing autobiographical material into something larger
than the stuff of a single, isolated life. That "no" at the

end of the poem, at the beginning of the pivotal year 1969, seems to me in some way the "no" of a whole generation of American women.

I'm fairly certain, though, that Jan didn't set out to speak for anyone but herself — or for anyone but that lost self whose life she painstakingly reveals here, detail by detail. By casting an objective, third-person eye on those details, she makes the act of writing also an act of reclamation and re-vision.

James Baker Hall was, in addition to being a poet and novelist, an acclaimed photographer. Much of his work in photography and poetry was concerned with recovering "a blasted childhood," as he put it, "without the aid of much memory." As a photographer, he worked with raw material from his family album— snapshots of his grandparents, his parents, and himself as a child— and then photographed those photographs and created double exposures and collages, using the inner eye to reveal in the present what had been hidden in the past. Some of the resulting images and Hall's poems can be found at: http://www.news-fromnowhere.com/jbhall01.html. Hall's process seems not unlike the process Mark Strand describes in

The Remains

I open the family album and look at myself as
    a boy. ...

I say my own name. I say goodbye,
The words follow each other downwind. ...
... I change and I am the same.
I empty myself of my life and my life remains.

Published Works Cited:

"The Maps," James Baker Hall, *The Total Light Process: New and Selected Poems* (Lexington, KY: The University Press of Kentucky), 2004

"The Remains," Mark Strand, *New Selected Poems* (New York, NY: Knopf) 2007

Poetry as Performance

by

M. B. McLatchey

Here is the opening stanza from a poem by Marilyn Chin that I have used in my writing classes:

How I Got That Name

An essay on assimilation

I am Marilyn Mei Ling Chin
Oh, how I love the resoluteness
of that first person singular
followed by that stalwart indicative
of "be," without the uncertain i-n-g
of "becoming." Of course,
the name had been changed
somewhere between Angel Island and the sea,
when my father the paperson
in the late 1950s
obsessed with a bombshell blond
transliterated "Mei Ling" to "Marilyn."

This poem works perfectly for us because Chin's examination of cultural assimilation instantly captures the interest of the large number of immigrant and second-language students that often characterize my classes. The tension that Chin portrays between *being* someone and *becoming* someone is often their tension as well, and it is a subject that deeply interests them. Beyond the subject of cultural assimilation, however, is a topic that I hope will become equally interesting to them—namely, the topic of poetic voice. This is a topic that we explore by examining the poem as both the written word as well as the performed word.

For an actual writing assignment, I begin by asking students to take Chin's title, "How I Got That Name" for a poem of their own making. So as not to over-direct their writing, I do not require them to take Chin's subtitle, "essay on assimilation"; nor, for this first round of writing, do I make them promise to any formal requirements beyond generating 10 lines of verse. We have not yet addressed issues of poetic technique, lineation, or stanza forms; therefore, at this stage, the majority of my students are casting whole thoughts or sentences into verse lines and producing a kind of paragraph in block form. Our objective at this point is simply to start talking in verse. When the students read their work aloud, we discuss the ideas that we hear, but our primary interest is in discovering the "I" who is speaking in the poem, the poetic voice with all of its nuances. Here is a sample of a student's verse essay:

> Maria, because it was easy
> to remember –
> my mother was Maria
> my Grandmother was
> Maria. So many Maria's
> that we all looked up
> when someone said our name –
> A tribe of women
> that seemed to be the same
> woman. I kept it to myself
> that I was not like them.
> Why upset history
> like that? After all,
> as my mother liked to say to me:
> *Who did I think I was*
> *anyway?*

In examining the ideas and attitudes in my students' poems, we spend the greater part of our time examining tone—specifically, we look at differences between factual statements, assumptions, biases and stereotypes, and figures of speech such as sarcasm and irony. In exploring mechanisms for communicating an emotion or an idea more powerfully, we explore devices in language such as simile, metaphor, and hyperbole or devices of poetry such as stanzas, lineation, punctuation and rhythm. Simply put, we consider the connection between form and feeling in poetry—but also, in all literary genres.

To deepen our examination of the link between poetic technique and voice, and to enhance our appreciation of the poem as performance, I ask my students to listen to a recording of Chin reading the poem "How I Got That Name." Almost naturally, while Chin reads her poem, my students' heads drop to look at the poem on the page. What are they looking for? They are looking for a match between the written word and the spoken word, between the technical arrangement on the page and the live dramatic performance— and what they find is a correspondence that seems achieved through art.

After hearing Chin read, our discussion naturally turns to issues regarding the written word as performance: inflection and emotional weight given to words and phrases, pacing and poetic techniques such as cadence, rhythm, and sound. They almost instantly notice the biting irony in the first line of Chin's poem, which seems to celebrate a "resoluteness," a definite identity, but in fact identifies an awkwardly hyphenated and unresolved identity: *I am Marilyn Mei Ling Chin.*

They also begin to hear the effects of repeated sounds and of verse line endings that underscore the speaker's embittered attitude and an unresolved "transliterated" identity, as when she describes how her father named her after Marilyn Monroe—a father, who "obsessed with a bombshell blond/ transliterated 'Mei Ling' to 'Marilyn.'"

In a second round of writing, students consciously apply some of the techniques that they noticed in Chin's poem, while also honing techniques that they have noticed in their own poems. They experiment with verse line breaks, cadence, and sound. Whole sentences that, in a first draft, were whole verse lines now become parsed for their cadence and for their emotional value.

Thus:

> "I am Juan Paul Jimenez
> My father had that name first"

becomes

> "I am Juan Paul Jimenez, named after
> my father, who was named after
> his father."

The objective, at this drafting stage, is to release ourselves from the expectation of linear development and from the logic of rhetoric and conscious thought that often characterizes prose writing and to instead engage with the play of language and unconscious thought that can characterize the poetic process. With each adjustment in verse lines that my students make, we discuss the degree to which message, voice, and tenor have been adjusted as well.

Often, my second-language students notice the degree to which Chin's experience with "transliteration" is theirs as well on a deeper level: namely, in the way that it applies to cadences and rhythms in their native languages that inevitably affect their use of the English language. To further explore this aspect of how cultural assimilation can create not just a merging of cultural values, but also a collision of linguistic and poetic cadences and forms, we might examine Chin's poems where she consciously merges Asian and Western verse forms.

Finally, to consider further the link between the performance of poetry and poetic techniques, we might also reverse this exercise by listening to recordings of poets first, and examining the written texts afterwards. While students listen to the poets perform their verses, they must jot down whatever words, ideas, and performance pauses they hear. In examining the written texts of these poems afterwards, our goal is to note the extent to which lineation, sound, rhythm, and other techniques guide performance and point to meaning. All of this is to offer students the opportunity to discover the vibrant and complex "I" that is at the center of their writing, while also gleaning from their writing exercises the link between form and feeling, the bond between the written word and the performed word.

Published Works Cited:

"How I Got that Name," Marilyn Chin, *The Phoenix Gone, the Terrace Empty* (Minneapolis, MN: Milkweed Editions), 1994

Accidental Writing

by

Doug Sutton-Ramspeck

For a long while I didn't fully realize that my creative writing students were producing their best work when they emulated Zen archers who accept that process is what matters and that aiming per se does not. But I am now convinced that, for most students, conscious effort is the enemy of invention. I'm not sure if this discovery is surprising or obvious, but again and again I have watched students lift the quality of their work when they stop trying so hard to do so. To that end I design my classes as a series of exercises, games, conversations, and playful activities meant to put everyone at ease, to help students no longer see writing a poem as like steering your car to a predetermined destination. I want them, instead, to envision the endeavor as more like lying on your back in a fast-moving river and letting the current carry you.

To begin, I hand my students a single note card. What they see on the blackboard while they are gripping that card in their hands is something like this:

A banana rotting slowly on a kitchen counter.

A sky turning ochre-colored at dusk.

I then ask them to write a line or two that is similar to the ones they are seeing—not similar in content, necessarily, but in structure. There are no restrictions, I tell them: no limitations, no wrong answers. I encourage them to jot down the first words that spring to mind.

"Just write," I say.

Their responses typically vary, of course, but here are a few I received last time from a class of beginning poetry-writing students:

A Hershey candy bar melting stickily in a backseat window.

A chair screeching slowly across the hardwood floor.

A thin brown grocery bag weighted down with peaches.

Once I have collected the note cards—this never takes more than a few minutes—I shuffle them like a deck of cards then announce to my students that, although they didn't realize it, they have been writing about a common theme of poets, returned to again and again, for good or for ill. Starting at the top of the deck, I read aloud:

> Love is a Hershey candy bar melting stickily in a backseat window.
> Love is a chair screeching slowly across the hardwood floor.
> Love is a thin brown grocery bag weighted down with peaches.

Some of these accidental lines are, of course, far more successful than others, and some are simply strange, but many elicit laughter or even that sudden intake of breath that occurs when something strikes a chord or a nerve.

At this point I ask my students to consider whether their answers would have been as interesting had I handed them note cards and asked them to fill in this blank: "Love is . . ." I doubt it, of course, and I let my students know that the one time I asked some students to serve as a "control group," the results were uniformly predictable and prosaic. Surprising your readers, I tell the class, means figuring out a way to surprise yourself.

I hope that by this time my students are relaxed and are feeling that odd confidence that comes from relinquishing conscious control over your creations, and I hope that they have come to trust—at least a little—the joys of writing blindly. So I put them to work on a rough draft of a poem, telling them I am going to write a topic on the blackboard, and the moment they see it, without thinking, they are going to start writing and keep writing, as rapidly as they can, without censoring any thought or impulse, until I ask them to stop. They should, I say, imagine themselves not as a writer but as an amanuensis: their job is to take down whatever chatter transpires in their heads, not to control it.

Two topics that always seem to elicit inventive and enthusiastic responses with beginning students are these:

Mermaid Cemetery Discovered
Zombies in Love

Ten minutes is almost always enough. By that time students have produced an impressive amount of material, and, in any case, have begun shaking their hands and rubbing their tired wrists. I ask for volunteers to read what they have produced, and first one student reads, then another, and eventually the floodgates open and almost all of them decide to share. One or two might hang back, but in another class or two they'll be joining in.

Here are two unedited samples of these ten-minute free-writings, one by a student who has completed an introductory poetry writing class, the other by a student who has never taken a creative writing class.

Victoria Gonzalez:

Each is marked by
dilapidated marble hovering
over a sandy bed.
Sea weed scattered throughout.

Stories to be told
have fallen upon plugged
ears. Light shines in, creating
rapidly changing spot lights.

There are no flowers. No
Statues of Christ. No
beaten stone path to
follow along.

The tombstones stand alone, united.
I stride forward for a
closer inspection.

A whirlpool of water
and color are about me.
I pop my head above the
surface gasping for air.

Alexis Alberts:

> Fins surfacing from underground as the rain
>   washes
> Dirt over itself.
> Men calling out to one another that they've
>   never
> Seen anything quite like it.
> They run to each other across the muddy,
>   sandy, swampy mess.
> Afraid that the motionless, half-decayed fish
>   bodies
> Would somehow regain control over them-
>   selves.
> The men, breathless from fear and sprinting,
> Meet in the middle.
> The very center of the eerily colorful home of
>   the dead.
> Human heads and fleshy, fishy things for
>   dresses.
> The men can't understand.

In both cases, it seems to me, the students have discovered some interesting possibilities, including "No / Statues of Christ. / No beaten stone path" and "fleshy, fishy things for dresses." I suspect that Victoria and Alexis might not have made these discoveries had they not launched into the unknown, had they not written to see where the writing went of its own volition.

But all of this is barely a beginning, of course, and it would be reasonable to ask what these students have "learned" so far about poetic technique, forms, terminology, and the rigors of revision. Fair enough. All of that will come next, of course, yet I am convinced that it is essential, even with these topics, not to lose sight of the fact that we should be appealing as much or more to a student's unconscious mind as to the conscious one.

So how, someone might sensibly ask, do you appeal to a student's unconscious mind when discussing image and detail, lineation and enjambment, the sonnet and the villanelle, and musical devices like alliteration, assonance, and consonance? It can be done, I believe, and I'll offer one example. Surely beginning students often resist the concrete image in favor of the bland and grand pronouncement, but rather than lecturing on the potential flaws of abstraction or hectoring my students to include more details in their work, I send them on a scavenger hunt. I ask them to find and make lists of details in nature books opened at random, in the contents of a backpack, in the particulars of a Degas painting projected on a screen, in a Google search prompted by a topic scrawled on a blackboard. Once students have collected their details, it is time to write—to write blindly—and to see where those details carry them.

The Extravagant Love Poem

by

Diane Lockward

One of my favorite and most successful activities is a variation of the *blazon*, a type of love poem dating back to 16th-century France. This activity works well with high school and college students as well as with adult writers, experienced or inexperienced.

A blazon is a poem of extravagant praise for the beloved, traditionally, a woman, but for our purposes, female or male. Such a poem includes a catalog of the beloved's body parts. Each of these parts is lavishly praised in metaphor. There are no rules regarding meter, rhyme, or number of lines. Depending on the academic level and intent of your group, you might introduce the blazon by looking at stanza 10 of Edmund Spenser's *Epithalamion*. If you do, be sure to note that Spenser's use of meter and rhyme is a choice, not a requirement.

But I like to jump right in with this contemporary blazon by Cecilia Woloch:

Blazon

—after Breton

My love with his hair of nightingales

With his chest of pigeon flutter, of gray doves preen-
ing themselves at dawn

With his shoulders of tender balconies half in shadow,
half in sun

My love with his long-boned thighs the map of Paris
of my tongue

With his ink-stained tongue, his tongue the tip

of a steeple plunged into milky sky

My love with his wishing teeth

With his fingers of nervous whispering, his fingers of
a boy

whose toys were cheap and broken easily

My love with his silent thumbs

With his eyes of a window smudged of a train that
passes in the night

With his nape of an empty rain coat
hung by the collar, sweetly bowed

My love with his laughter of an empty stairwell, rain
all afternoon

With his mouth the deepest flower to which

I have ever put my mouth

Typically, students first notice the use of repetition, thus providing a good opportunity to introduce the term *anaphora* and discuss how the device functions in the poem as the key structural component, line by line laying down the bones that support the catalog of body parts—hair, chest, shoulders, thighs, tongue, teeth, fingers, thumbs, eyes, mouth. The anaphora also adds rhythm, a steady drumbeat, which Woloch enhances by alternating the "My love" lines with the "With his" ones.

Students should also notice the absence of a narrative line. One of the virtues of the blazon is its lyricism; using this form in workshop helps story-bound poets move away from narrative. The poem does not even contain complete sentences or conventional punctuation. In fact, it's only in the last line that we have a subject-verb construction. I like to end the discussion by asking students to select their favorite metaphors. In doing so, they can't help but notice that metaphors do more than convey ideas, conjure images, and express emotion; they also delight us.

Then we do this exercise which employs some of the elements of Woloch's blazon.

Ask students to begin a first line with "You are my . . ." For this quick draft, do not worry about body parts.

Now ask students to complete the first line by identifying the beloved as

1. a dessert (e.g., You are my crème brûlée.)

Instruct students to skip a line. They should also skip a line after each of the following additions.

At the beginning of the next line, students again write "You are my . . ." and then

complete line 2 by identifying the beloved as

2. a beverage

Continue as above through the remaining lines, calling out the categories one at a time and reminding students to skip one line between each metaphor.

3. bird

4. jewel

5. tree

6. flower

7. body of water

8. a category of their own choosing

9. Ask students to end the poem by repeating line #1 but with an embellishment, e.g., You are my crème brûlée, my jiggly pudding, my sweet sugar topping.

This part of the activity takes mere minutes. Now allow additional time for students to add details in the open spaces and to weave in a catalog of body parts. This may necessitate changing the "You are my" anaphora, but that's fine. Students should be encouraged to let line lengths vary.

Revision Strategies

Ask students to rearrange the order of the lines.

Ask them also to consider changing from present to past tense. For some students, this adjustment will be a dramatic eye opener as time and tone completely shift.

Also ask students to decide if they want to keep the last line or end with one of the unique metaphors. Some will like the neatness of the circular structure; others will like the impact of a startling closing metaphor.

Ask students to polish the language. It's a lyric; it should sing.

Finally, you may want to discuss whether or not an attribution is necessary. If you look at André Breton's "Free Union," you'll see that Woloch's debt to that poet is clear. An attribution is necessary. But if your students have strayed far from Woloch's poem, it's possible that no attribution is needed.

From here, we move onto the *anti-blazon*. Working counter to what we've done before invariably opens up exciting possibilities. For an example from earlier days, you might look at Shakespeare's Sonnet 130. Or you might get right to Kim Addonizio's poem as an example.

You

You were a town with one pay phone and some-
    one else was using it.

You were an ATM temporarily unable to dis-
    pense cash.

You were an outdated link and the server was
    down.

You were invisible to the naked eye.

You were the two insect parts per million allowed
    in peanut butter.

You were a car wash that left me as dirty as when
    I pulled in.

You were twenty rotting bags of rice in the hold
    of a cargo plane sitting on the runway in a
    drought-riddled country.

You were one job opening for two hundred applicants and you paid minimum wage.

You were grateful for my submission but you just couldn't use it.

You weren't a Preferred Provider.

You weren't giving any refunds.

You weren't available for comment.

Your grave wasn't marked so I wandered the cemetery for hours, part of the grass, part of the crumbling stones.

Addonizio's poem contains some of the elements of Woloch's poem, but varies them. For example, the poem uses anaphora, but while Woloch's speaker told us *about* her beloved, Addonizio's directly addresses him—as students did in their own blazons. The repeated "you" thus becomes an indictment of the former beloved (or is he former?). Addonizio switches to opposition as her speaker tells us what the *you* was *not*. "You were" becomes "You weren't." This switch breaks the pattern of the poem and knocks predictability on its ear. More importantly, the tone now shifts as, line by line, the poem ceases to be funny. There is a catalog but of random items rather than of body parts. Addonizio also uses extravagant metaphors, but they are hardly flattering.

Repeat the same activity, but now ask students to create metaphors that express anger and unhappiness, e.g., "You were the soufflé that wouldn't rise." If you want variety, you can change the categories.

Depending on the length of your workshop session, you might get both activities into one day. But it's also possible, given shorter sessions, to do the blazon one day and the anti-blazon the following day. Another option is to read both poems together and then give students a choice as to how they want to approach the activity. Sometimes I compress the activity and call it "The Ten-Minute Love Poem"— especially if we're near Valentine's Day. It is even possible to exclude the definition of blazon and the examples and simply present the activity as one that capitalizes on metaphors.

The step-by-step procedure might at first glance seem at odds with the spontaneity and free flow of ideas we associate with creativity. If there is some initial resistance, that in itself can be creative. The collision between what writers instinctively want to do and what they are asked to do will almost certainly open up new territory. Most writers, however, willingly go with me through the activity. In fact, as we move along, anticipation builds for what is coming next.

Published Works Cited:

"You," Kim Addonizio, *Lucifer at the Starlite* (New York, NY: W.W. Norton), 2009.

"Blazon," Cecilia Woloch, *Carpathia* (New York, NY: BOA Editions), 2009.

Mapping the Line

by

Bruce Guernsey

Some time ago, while having dinner with a farmer friend and his wife, the topic of poetry came up. They wanted to know more about it and asked me this simple yet very profound question: "So what's the difference between poetry and regular writing anyway?"

I poured myself another glass of wine and paused, not knowing how to explain without sounding like a pedant. I wanted to answer as simply as they had asked, and no doubt it was the vino that helped: "Well," I said, "I guess it's the difference between singing and speaking."

In a way, this little exchange between my friends and me is repeated every semester when beginning poets walk into an introductory course in writing. To get them to "sing" and not "speak" is the goal of the course. How to do that is the challenge, and I've come up with a writing exercise that you might want to try.

It's called the "map poem" and involves the distinction between the line and the sentence. The tendency of most young poets is to write in sentences, in what my friends called "regular writing." Line breaks occur for reasons of syntax. As a result, each line is a grammatical unit, usually clauses—both dependent and independent—or a series of prepositional phrases.

To show you what I mean, here's a stanza about the coming of spring in Alaska. It's from the poem "And When the Green Man Comes" by John Haines that I've written out as prose: "His eyes are blind with April, his breath distilled of butterflies and bees, and in his beard the maggot sings."

When I ask the students to write this in lines, here's what I invariably get:

> His eyes are blind with April,
> his breath distilled
> of butterflies and bees,
> and in his beard
> the maggot sings.

But here's how Haines broke the lines:

His eyes are blind
with April,
his breath distilled
of butterflies
and bees, and in his beard
the maggot sings.

The students' version pays little-to-no attention to sound and rhythm. The line breaks are grammatical units of sense, which is "correct" in "regular writing." Sense is the goal of the sentence, as we've all been taught. A sentence *is* a complete thought. But a line in poetry is often not, and even when it is, such as the first line of Haines' actual poem, we are also hearing those long vowel sounds that are emphasized by the two-beat, iambic line. His version also lets us hear the wonderful liquid sounds of spring because they occur at the end of lines. And how wonderful, too, is Haines' separation of butterflies and bees, of creatures of silence from those of sound.

My map poem exercise forces the students away from speaking and more toward singing. I take a road map of Illinois and hold it open. The first thing we do is to look at the state—at its shape, that is. The way you should a poem, I believe—look at its figure on the page. Poems and states do have shapes, and when I was a kid, I learned the states by learning what they looked like, just the way you can tell a Dickinson poem from some lines by Whitman.

A poem occupies a very different space on the page than does "regular writing," and lines are what define both the boundaries of a poem and of our states. A look at Illinois shows how nature shaped the east and west borders, but there are no straight lines in nature. That one between Illinois and its cheese-head neighbor to the north was made by legislation.

Thus, opening the map—and this applies to any state—gives you a chance to talk about shaping. But living in east central Illinois does give me the added advantage of looking out the window to the fields around us, though even if you don't live out here, you can still write the word *versere* on the board. It is Latin for "to turn" and has an agricultural meaning to it. When my farmer neighbor reaches the end of his field, he turns his John Deere around and starts a new row, just as Virgil's friends did their oxen. Little does my neighbor know, however, that he is doing what a poet does in making "verse."

Which brings me back to the map assignment in line-making. I ask the students to write a poem using only the names of cities and towns, counties and rivers that they find on the map. No other parts of speech are allowed, including articles and prepositions. Nothing but the proper nouns on that map.

They can shape the poem any way they like, and some get quite inventive, often trying to duplicate the shape of the state itself or using the compass or a highway to arrange the names. I discourage such methods of shaping, however, because I want them to be using their ears here, and their foot to tap with. I want them to be listening to the vowels and consonants and to the rhythms that result, and to break their lines for reasons of sound. By taking "sense" away, the students are forced to fall back on something far more primitive than the complete thought.

This assignment is not only an exercise in breaking lines. Because of our unique history as a country, "mapping the line" is also a lesson in the origins of American English. To show you what I mean, here's my own version of a map poem which was published in a special edition of *Sou'Wester* called "Illinois Authors," edited by Robert Wrigley:

Adam's Task

Rockford Rocktop Rock Falls Boulder Hill
Fishhook Passport Cave in Rock Carlock
Blue Mound Blackstone Pinkstaff Bigfoot

Bearsdale Shawneetown Little Indian Buf-
falo Hart

Cairo Crete Sparta Thebes
El Paso De Soto Sorento Peru
Dundee DesPlains Bourbonnais Champaign
Zion Athens Paris Waterloo

Oblong Normal Winkle Dix
Colp Kell Fults Gays
Red Bud Crossroads Lick Creek Round
Knob
Bigneck Beardstown Bunkum Bruce

Pawnee Pawpaw Pocahontas Pontiac
Mowequa Wapella Wataga Kewanee
Tiskilwa Watseka Chicago Chebanse
Toluca Tonica Iuka Kankakee

Hurricane Marrowbone Vermillion Kickapoo
Embarras Wabash Ohio Mississippi

Have fun with this exercise. I use it in literature
courses, too, especially freshman genre sections. The
students enjoy doing it. And if you share my own map
poem with them, be sure to mention the famous, and
actual, headline from a local paper's social page a few
years ago: "Oblong Man Marries Normal Woman."

Published Works Cited:

"Adam's Task," Bruce Guernsey, *Sou'Wester* (Vol. 21, Nos. 1 and 2) Fall, 1993

"And When the Green Man Comes," John Haines, *The Owl in the Mask of the Dreamer* (St. Paul, MN: Graywolf Press), 1994

Metaphor as Form

by

David Baker

Metaphor is the fundamental trope of poetry and comes in a variety of flavors—simile, metonymy, personification, and so on. But what happens when we think of metaphor as the form of an entire poem?

I have developed a simple assignment for my students that explores this question. My goal is to steer my students away from their tendency to write a poem "about" a single subject, to steer them away from the over-determination of subject matter and away from too singular or self-enclosed a narrative: to steer them toward complexity and connection—the leap of likeness.

Here is the actual assignment:

Write a short poem (limited to one page) in which you find two components or images, which may have little to do with each other, and fuse them; make them depend entirely on each other, or reveal something fundamental about each other. Make one part of the metaphor disclose something about the other.

As an example, consider this very simple, very effective poem by Jane Kenyon called "Three Small Oranges." Even the formal construction of her poem is simple, with one dominant trope and story per stanza. Notice how efficiently one part of the metaphor becomes embedded in the other. Kenyon knows that combining two things can make a third.

> My old flannel nightgown, the elbows out,
> one shoulder torn . . . Instead of putting it
> away with the clean wash, I cut it up
> for rags, removing the arms and opening
> their seams, scissoring across the breast
> and upper back, then tearing the thin
> cloth of the body into long rectangles.
> Suddenly an immense sadness . . .
>
> Making supper, I listen to news
> from the war, of torture where the air
> is black at noon with burning oil,
> and of a market in Baghdad, bombed
> by accident, where yesterday an old man
> carried in his basket a piece of fish
> wrapped in paper and tied with string,
> and three small hard green oranges.

Kenyon's poem represents the most elementary version of my assignment. One stanza contains one narrative and the second stanza contains the second, separate narrative. It's a good way to see how metaphor may work in the large scale: The two parts of the overall metaphor become the form of the entire poem. I can imagine that Kenyon could have written a whole poem about the story in the first stanza—the story of American good-fortune. We make rags out of our own clothes! How lucky we must be. And I can imagine that she might write a whole poem about the first Gulf war, the terror of modern warfare and the insistent going-on of daily life even in war. I infer in her second stanza that the old man does not survive the next day's bombing. After all, he did his gathering "yesterday," and the suggestion of those "hard green oranges" is that they will never turn ripe and orange.

To me, the magic happens when the first episode morphs into the second. I feel the profound slippage from one landscape (interior, domestic, safe, fortunate) into the second (outside, faraway, perilous, sparse). I would not necessarily see these things if the poem were two separate poems. I certainly wouldn't see the powerful connection in the two parts. What connection? Look at Kenyon's choice in the first stanza; every gesture is quietly violent, a motion of dismantling, taking-apart, moving outward, as the "body" of the garment is disembodied or blown apart. But in the second stanza the gestures are of gathering, holding-together, tying-up—cognitive opposites of the action itself. That's the magic of the simple strategy. She found a way to link the two scenarios.

If you find this interesting, you might look at other similar poems where the two fundamental parts or stories are presented in two separate stanzas: "Ex Machina" by Lisel Mueller, "A Comparison" and "Trash" by Ruth Stone, "Astronomy" by Albert Goldbarth, "Death's Portrait" by Chase Twichell. Even these famous classic poems use this basic formula: "The Emperor of Ice Cream" by Wallace Stevens, "When I Heard the Learn'd Astronomer" by Walt Whitman.

The next step to this exercise is to embed one of a poem's narratives within the other. This is a slightly more complex formulation of metaphor-as-form. Here is T. R. Hummer's "Where You Go When She Sleeps" from *The Angelic Orders*.

> What is it when a woman sleeps, her head
>   bright
> In your lap, in your hands, her breath easy
>   now as though it had never been
> Anything else, and you know she is dreaming,
>   her eyelids

Jerk, but she is not troubled, it is a dream

That does not include you, but you are not
    troubled either,

It is too good to hold her while she sleeps, her
    hair falling

Richly on your hands, shining like metal, a color

That when you think of it you cannot name,
    as though it has just

Come into existence, dragging you into the
    world in the wake

Of its creation, out of whatever vacuum you
    were in before,

And you are like the boy you heard of once
    who fell

Into a silo full of oats, the silo emptying from
    below, oats

At the top swirling in a gold whirlpool, a
    bright eddy of grain, the boy,

You imagine, leaning over the edge to see it,
    the noon sun breaking

Into the center of the circle he watches, hot
    on his back, burning,

And he forgets his father's warning, stands on
    the edge, looks down,

The grain spinning, dizzy, and when he falls
    his arms go out, too thin

For wings, and he hears his father's cry some-
    where, but is gone

Already, down into a gold sea, spun deep into
    the heart of the silo,

And when they find him, his mouth, his
    throat, his lungs
Full of the gold that took him, he lies still, not
    seeing the world
Through his body but through the deep rush
    of grain
Where he has gone and can never come back,
    though they drag him
Out, his father's tears bright on both their
    faces, the farmhands
Standing by blank and amazed—you touch
    that unnamable
Color in her hair and you are gone into what
    is not fear or joy
But a whirling of sunlight and water and air
    full of shining dust
That takes you, a dream that is not of you but
    will let you
Inside itself if you love enough, and will not,
    will never let you go.

By putting part two literally inside part one, Hummer suggests the profound relationship of the love poem to the elegy. We tend to regard these rhetorical forms of lyric poetry to be opposite. One is about love, one is about death. Hummer shows us otherwise, that the impulses are profound, basic, and intimately linked; they contain each other. To be this deeply in love is, in part, to lose one's self, to die into one's lover.

But look at other features here, other aspects that connect the two parts of Hummer's overall metaphor. This big poem with very long lines is just one sentence and one stanza! Why? Perhaps because we literally run out of breath reading it, the way the boy asphyxiates in the grain silo. The long lines tumble, perhaps the way we "fall" in love. Certainly the boy falls; certainly something takes his breath away. Notice how the woman's long golden hair becomes the swirl and color and richness of the pouring grain. The story of Rapunzel meets the story of Icarus. Hummer seems to have made these discoveries as he connected the two separate stories.

Finally, here is one even more subtle application of metaphor-as-form. This is Jane Hirshfield's poem, "Three Foxes by the Edge of the Field at Twilight" from *The Lives of the Heart*.

> One ran,
> her nose to the ground,
> a rusty shadow
> neither hunting nor playing.
>
> One stood; sat; lay down; stood again.
>
> One never moved,
> except to turn her head a little as we walked.
> Finally we drew too close,

and they vanished.
The woods took them back as if they had
    never been.

I wish I had thought to put my face to the
    grass.

But we kept walking,
speaking as strangers do when becoming
    friends.

There is more and more I tell no one,
strangers nor loves.
This slips into the heart
without hurry, as if it had never been.

And yet, among the trees, something has
    changed.

Something looks back from the trees,
and knows me for who I am.

    In Hirshfield's poem the two primary narratives
are more fully interwoven than in Hummer's poem.
They "slip" in and out of each other. We have the
narrative of spotting the foxes (three of them!) at a
wood's edge and watching them eventually trot away.
And we have the subtle story of the two people. Are
they friends, are they falling in love? What do these two

stories have to do with each other? But I find an even more ghostly presence in this poem. This is the poem's special drama to me—the very quiet narrative here of privacy and secrecy. Here, to me, is the richest paradox of the poem; as we grow older, as we have more and more relationships, we grow hungrier for privacy, for the intimacy that one can feel only with one's self.

Hirshfield makes her poem, then, not of two but three parts. And look how she provides linkage: by the similarity of the stories, but more so by her unifying tone and the magic of her repetitions. The foxes vanish, just as something "slips into the heart"; the foxes are on the edge of woods, just as the couple seems on the edge of something large and shifting; the foxes are taken back into the trees "as if they had never been," just as the speaker's self-knowledge slips into the privacy of her heart, "as if it had never been." These echoes provide the means for Hirshfield's profound connections, the musical linkage of the parts of her lovely metaphor.

From here, perhaps the assignment invites students—or yourself—to open out further, toward more and more complexity, more and more subtlety. But my point is simple. As I tell my students, it's not enough to have a good story to make a poem. It is not enough to have one good image, or one good idea. You need two. Or three. Four . . .

Published Works Cited:

"Three Small Oranges," Jane Kenyon, *Otherwise: New & Selected Poems* (St. Paul, MN: Graywolf Press), 1996.

"Three Foxes by the Edge of the Field at Twilight," Jane Hirshfield, *The Lives of the Heart* (New York, NY: Harper Perennial), 1997.

"Where You Go When She Sleeps," T. R. Hummer, *The Angelic Orders* (Baton Rouge, LA: Louisiana State University Press), 1982.

Beginning with *Some God* . . .

by

Miho Nonaka

As a college student, I became accustomed to poetry assignments that lacked concrete guidelines. Out of respect for students' creative freedom or mere personal exhaustion, my professors' instructions tended to be more impressionistic than literal. I still remember one of my first workshop assignments: *Write any poem by next week, but PLEASE, don't talk about love, death, or being lonely.* When I started teaching, I was embarrassingly slow to understand students' legitimate need for specific protocols before they could invite their respective muses. The writing exercise I will share here is one of the earlier, still amorphous ones I improvised, but the one that ended up helping me and my students better understand the essential impetus of lyric poetry.

After my students had read Pablo Neruda's manifesto, "Toward an Impure Poetry" and discussed what would make a poem that "smells of lilies and urine," I gave the following assignment:

Write a poem that starts with the first line of a poem by a mystery American poet: "By the roots of my hair some god got hold of me." The rest is up to you, but think of developing it in terms of contradictions: beautiful and unbeautiful, pure and impure, the "high and low" images, contexts or sentiments.

I didn't disclose to the students that the line was from "The Hanging Man " by Sylvia Plath, a slender piece, ruthlessly condensed to six lines from the material that could have easily given birth to half a dozen poems.

By the roots of my hair some god got hold of me.
I sizzled in his blue volts like a desert prophet.

The nights snapped out of sight like a lizard's eyelid:
A world of bald white days in a shadeless socket.

A vulturous boredom pinned me in this tree.
If he were I, he would do what I did.

Now I realize that I could have added one more directive, something along the lines of "organize your poem in unrhymed couplets," in order to emphasize the dialectic content of the assignment. But I still hadn't wrapped my mind around Plath's poem itself; its first line simply kept haunting me as a seductive starting point for the unknown, the magnetic pull of Alice's rabbit hole. As a rule, I discourage beginning writers from using abstractions by invoking the cult of "vivid, concrete details." Even without a capital G, inclusion of a nebulous entity like "some god" could be problematic, but I liked the casual ambiguity of "some," and the fact that it's juxtaposed with "the roots of my hair" gives an appropriate nod to my instruction about mixing the "high and low" images.

The class cringed at my announcement as if I had just hurled Zeus's thunderbolt at them, but this assignment forced the students not only to tackle with the concept of hybrid reality, but also to come up with poetic lines that suggest both complexity and a departure from their usual writing style.

One student began his poem with "By the roots of my hair some god got hold of me / and pulled me down to his level." He reverses traditional hierarchy by having his speaker stooped to "some god"; its irony makes for a shrewd, gripping start.

Another student, whose territory was mostly narrative poems based on real life events, managed to let go of her scaffolding instinct as a conscientious storyteller. I will quote the first two stanzas:

> By the roots of my hair some god got hold of me
> not God, but an ancient Loki
> or his offspring
>
> yanked me down,
> ground my bones
> inside the sidewalk

The speaker quickly redefines "some god" as the classic trickster or his modern descendant and simply lists his acts of violence without explaining why this is happening or what the speaker herself is feeling. The student had never taken such a jagged, unapologetic move in her previous poems, often organized in stable quatrains of equal-length lines. Plath's daring opening forced the student to follow its act by taking her first leap of lyric intensity and distillation, resulting in the speaker's symbolic descent from the realm of ancient mythology to the stark scene of "my bones" against the quotidian "sidewalk."

The third student turned in a poem entitled "Earthbound." Its first stanza establishes the poem's setting and its emotional climate brilliantly:

> By the roots of my hair some god got hold of me;
> I had pocketed my pills and walked toward morning
> on banks of Dismal Creek.

I admire the student's choice of "Dismal Creek" over "a dismal creek"; the speaker's dark mood turns an arbitrary stream into a proper noun and a definitive place name that exists only on her psychic geography. By contrast, the identity of "some god" remains unclear throughout the poem, except that it's a female god who revokes the speaker's self-destructive impulse to overdose by making her crawl back home. Then, the poem takes a surprising turn at the end:

> The banks of Dismal Creek seeking peace—
> an empty Buddha kind—
> my empty Buddha mind—floating water on Earth.

By definition, "Buddha" is not a god but a state of being. The poem's equation of the speaker's devastated, hollow self with enlightenment becomes a sort of ironic hymn, "floating water on Earth," which is reminiscent of the final image you would find in

"Tulips," another poem by Sylvia Plath. In the wintry hospital, Plath's worn-out speaker calls herself "nobody" and "a nun," bleached of her identity and past attachments, and she becomes increasingly terrorized by a vivid reminder of life, an unwelcome gift of tulips that are "too excitable." The poem concludes with unexpected tears on the speaker's cheeks: "The water I taste is warm and salt, like the sea, / And comes from a country far away as health."

In the end, the students and I came away from this writing exercise with a deepened awareness of the consuming energy that underlies the making of lyric. What is at the source of its motion is a reckless belief in the oracular status of subjectivity, an illegitimate passion to enshrine personal feeling in the most heightened and melodious pattern of language conceivable. In this way, each god, each force of human emotion, must be laboriously and artfully distanced from the poet's self.

My requirement of starting a poem with such a daunting line might have made the students' experience more burdensome than called for. (At least I had relented from giving them the opening of Rilke's mythic elegies, "Who, if I cried out, would hear me among the angels' hierarchies?") I acknowledge that not every angel in the lyric universe has to be "terrifying." Plath's "Hanging Man" is its own beast, a uniquely explosive mixture of "lilies" and "urine." What Neruda might call the "impurity" of her poem is a result of matching the ultimate opposites and making their union appear inevitable: what is deemed sacred with the profane, life with the "vulturous boredom," and finally, "some god" with an ungodly impulse of self-murder.

Published Works Cited:

"The Hanging Man," Sylvia Plath, *Ariel* (New York, NY: Harper & Row), 1966.

Three Exercises for Free Verse

by

Wesley McNair

Here are three exercises for lively ways of teaching the elements of free verse. I have used them dozens of times in my classes on poetry writing to good effect.

1. The first helps introduce line-breaking. After explaining to your class that free verse, unlike poetry in rhyme and meter, is written for the page and makes its appeal to the eye as well as to the ear, pass out four or five free verse poems and discuss how their line breaks convey special meanings. Have them read, for instance, William Carlos Williams's "The Term," Mary Oliver's "August," W.S. Merwin's "The Name of the Air," or any other poems that are artfully broken into lines. Ask some general questions like, "How does this poem look like what it says, or how it thinks?" Or: "How

does the poet give emphasis to important phrases or end words by breaking lines?" Or: "How does the use of space around the poem and its stanzas contribute to its meaning?" If these questions seem too theoretical for the class at first, save them for later and begin by pointing out two or three especially effective breaks and asking how they benefit the poem.

After the discussion is complete, turn to the exercise. Read W.C. Williams's "Poem" aloud. Then do a second, slower reading, telling your students to copy the poem down as prose. ("Poem" is the well-known piece about the cat stepping carefully over the jam closet.) Once they've finished the copying, have them try writing out the lines of the original, giving them only two clues: that it's in four stanzas, and that each is three lines long.

Compare the results, asking individual students to read their line breaks aloud and give the reasons why they broke as they did. The goal should not be to reproduce the original exactly, but to make the class think harder about how line-breaking works. This approach will give you the chance to praise your students even when they might be at odds with the original, offering them encouragement as they risk their first attempts with the line. As discussion goes along, apply the principal of cost and benefit, making the class see that a good line break must be measured against its possible cost to the next line, or to some desired effect of cadence or meaning in the passage as a whole. After hearing from five or six students, conclude by reading Williams's poem line by line so the class take it down and learn through their pens, asking for comments every so often about the effectiveness of the original line or stanza division.

Repeat this exercise with other free verse poems—or excerpts from them— transcribed as prose. To your own possible models, add James Laughlin's "The Child," Denise Levertov's "Six Variations, iii," Mark Strand's "Reasons for Moving," or David Wagoner's "The Recital."

2. Here's an exercise that will help your students appreciate the effect of images in poetry and sharpen their skills as image-makers at the same time. Explain to the class that poetry is a coded language that depends utterly on the image. Illustrate the point by reading Theodore Roethke's "My Papa's Waltz" aloud and asking the following questions: "What clue do we have to the height of the boy in the poem, and therefore to his relative age?" "What does the father do for work?" "What single image reveals the mother in the poem,

and what meanings do you find in it?" "What is the relationship between the son and the father?" Through such questions, the class will see how suggestive and important images can be in a poem. Try also, say, Jane Kenyon's "Three Small Oranges," or James Wright's "Lying in a Hammock at William Duffy's Farm," or perhaps Charles Simic's "Butcher Shop."

Next, split your students into groups of three, asking each group to write down whatever images may come to mind in response to one of the following questions:

> What articles are left unsold at the end of the yard sale?
>
> What was under the refrigerator when you moved it?
>
> What's in the kitchen's junk drawer?
>
> What has been placed for show on the front lawn of a certain rural house in the boondocks?
>
> What's been collected in the backyard of a certain rural house?

Afterward, have the groups cut their lists down to four essential images, then arrange the resulting list in climactic order, placing the most dramatic or interesting image in the third or fourth position and building the other entries around it. This activity will show students how even a small poem can be shaped into an arc. It will also, with a little luck, deliver them a short and compelling poem. Conclude the exercise with a class reading.

At some point during the group work, caution your students against using adjectives, which can end up "telling" the reader rather than "showing" him or her. For an illustration, discuss the difference between this image for the junk drawer: "a discarded tool," and this one: "half a pair of plyers"; or between this image for the rural backyard: "an old, rusted-out car" and this one: "a Cadillac on blocks with bullet holes." Students drawn to adjectives should ask themselves what the thing they are describing looked like in the first place to inspire the adjectives.

3. This final exercise has to do with syntax. Good poems depend on an engaging process of thinking. As Robert Frost once said, a poem is "a think." When our students turn to contemporary poetry for guidance in their syntax, they often get bad lessons, since today's poems tend to be written in a loose grammar. So the most common sentence in contemporary work starts off with a subject and verb, following up with phrases or clauses. Thus the sentence lacks all suspense and drama, winding down rather than winding up.

The aim of this exercise is to show students the effect a dramatic sentence can have. Begin once more with a reading of poems, each of them written in one periodic sentence, with a lengthy introductory clause and a verb that is delayed till the very end. Possibilities are John Keats's sonnet, "When I Have Fears That I May Cease To Be,"or Walt Whitman's "When I Heard the Learned Astronomer," or Robert Francis's wonderful but lesser-known "Emergence." After the reading, ask the class to write a poem in the manner of "Emergence," beginning with an introductory "if" clause. Like "Emergence," the in-class poem should follow the general pattern of complications or difficulties leading to achievement – or to some qualified achievement. Its lines should be carefully broken to stress the sentence's dramatic, rising action.

Encourage reasonably long introductory clauses and short main clauses for the in-class exercise, but add that to avoid grammatical confusion, students should use no more than two if's in the introductory part of their sentence. Possible topics:

Humorous:

Getting out of a traffic ticket ("If you can put aside the shock/ of the whirling, blue/ lights in your rear view/ and...etc.")

Getting through a ghastly poetry reading

Picking out an outfit with your mother

Winning an argument with your boyfriend, girl-friend, spouse

Getting through the first week of a diet

Serious:

Surviving a particular grief or heartbreak

Surviving a difficult childhood or parenthood

Dealing with a certain kind of rejection (your choice of which)

Finding fulfillment (your choice of which)

Finishing, despite the obstacles, a poem

Like the other in-class exercises I've suggested here, this one should be followed by reading aloud. Students who complete the exercise may not end up with a full-fledged poem, but through their work with the syntax of delay, they will better understand how they can create the dramatic tension that is essential to poetry in free verse, the line tugging back on the sentence, and the restless sentence slipping away.

Framing the House

by

Todd Davis

In order to help students begin to see that good writing is often about the "things" of this world and not its abstractions, I ask them to write a poem about where they live, one in which they use only nouns that we can taste or smell or touch or hear or see.

To show them what I mean I use several poems to get us started. The first is Robert Cording's "Why I Live Here," because in its opening lines it provides a rudimentary form that students find approachable:

> Because the view is always partial,
> small-paned, the sky parceled out by trees.
>
> Because I like the grey and brown birds
> and how they flit in and out of my vision

in the grey and brown woods,
endless versions of what can and cannot be seen.

And because I like the mystery of an old truck
that suddenly appears in the middle

of these roadless, second-growth woods,
a maple sapling growing from the windshield,

its backseat a storehouse for nuts,
a chickadee bathing on its caved-in roof.

Students quickly perceive how Cording's use of *anaphora*—the repetition of the "because" clause—creates a structure that helps him answer the title's rhetorical prompt. At the same time, they also witness the poet calling up the "things" that litter the world around his house: "grey and brown birds"; "an old truck"; "a maple sapling growing from the windshield"; "a chickadee bathing." At this point I ask them to make a list of 20 objects—animate or inanimate—that surround their houses or apartments.

As we get started, I keep pushing them to speak with greater specificity. Here are some artifacts that students have listed: "a Waste Management dumpster"; "the rusty white sign of the Juniata Original Italian Pizza restaurant"; "a male cardinal in the limb of a hemlock"; "a neighbor's clothesline with six ivory-colored bras waving in the wind"; "a half-empty bottle of blue Gatorade tossed to the side of Wopsononock Boulevard"; and "a golden retriever squatting over a patch of yellowing grass."

After making these lists, we visit another poet in his domicile and try to answer whether his concerns about his house are the same as Cording's. In "Where I Live," Billy Collins describes the manner in which his house is situated:

> The house sits at one end of a two-acre trapezoid.
> There is a wide lawn, a long brick path,
> rhododendrons, and large, heavy maples.

Geometry aside, most of my students believe Collins is up to something that's similar to Cording. But part way through the poem, Collins shifts from simple description of his house's location and its wide array of accoutrements to the physical acts he performs within his home space.

> Tomorrow early, I will drive down
> and talk to the stonecutter,
> but today I am staying home,

standing at one window, then another,

or putting on a jacket

and wandering around outside

or sitting in a chair

watching the trees full of light-green buds

under the low hood of the sky.

Upon their first reading, students will sometimes ask why Collins bothers to tell us about such mundane actions—that is, until the poet's revelation of his father's death:

This is the first good rain to fall

since my father was buried last week,

and even though he was very old,

I am amazed at how the small drops

stream down the panes of glass,

as usual,

gathering,

as they always have,

in pools on the ground.

Collins teaches us to communicate the weight of grief without ever using the word; a fine example to support William Carlos Williams' contention that there are no ideas but in things.

And this leads us to the second step in the exercise. The things we notice in our lived space and that we choose to include in our poems will differ based upon our emotional mood or psychological state. In addition, a certain object can change its emotional tone in a poem, yet still be the same physical object in the "real" world. At this point, students take their list of objects and write next to each one the emotion they associate with it. They do not have to explain why they associate that emotion with that particular object, but in simply doing a quick Rorschach test they begin to perceive the emotional weight of the words that will serve as the building blocks of their poems.

Here are students' emotional responses from the previous list: "a Waste Management dumpster" = "nasty, smelly despair"; "the rusty white sign of the Juniata Original Italian Pizza restaurant" = "comfort/safety"; "a male cardinal in the limb of a hemlock" = "sex/lust"; "six ivory-colored bras waving in the wind" = "love from/for my mom and sister"; "a half-empty bottle of blue Gatorade tossed to the side of Wopsononock Boulevard" = "anger"; and "a golden retriever squatting over a patch of yellowing grass" = "laughter/joy".

Finally, we turn our attention to Jack Ridl's "Framing the Morning" in order to examine how our work as writers is similar to the work of painters. In the poem, Ridl offers an instance in which the writer must decide what will be included inside the frame of the poem and what, often reluctantly, must be left outside the frame. Again, the subject is the writer's domestic space.

> Next to the sofa, books: an atlas, the poems of John
> Clare, a guide to wild flowers.

> The sudden lash of light across the kitchen window-
> sill—
> the silver top of the pepper mill
> the pale yellow of the egg timer
> the sparkle of whisks.

Like a still-life painter, Ridl draws our eye to the objects in the path of his gaze. These are the most mundane things—a sofa, some books, kitchen implements—but because they are framed by the poem, because other objects that certainly existed in these rooms are not included, what survives begins to shine, to take on the aspect of a certain luminosity.

Perhaps what's most interesting is Ridl's refusal to offer any commentary; his doggedness in not introducing an agent of action. He moves from stanza to stanza, placing the thing itself before our eyes.

Toast. Currant jam. Coffee with cream.
The chipped plate with the half-moon painted in its center.

Out by the swatch of jewelweed and daylilies, two chairs.
    The light falls across them,
        their shadows growing longer.
The morning paper, folded open to the crossword.
    On the porch, a blanket and binoculars.

I ask students what they "feel" as they move through Ridl's poem. Without the pressure or anxiety to make the poem "mean," they discuss their emotional experience, and they discover that these objects resonate with them, that the order the objects are placed in actually makes a difference. (Sometimes we even play a game of cut and paste to see what happens when we put these objects in a different order or leave some out.) This part of the exercise helps them understand what a still-life painting has to offer, and how that art form might inform their own poetic practices.

Which brings us to the final outcome. Gathering our lists of objects, considering the emotional weight we attach to them, borrowing the idea of anaphora as an organizing principle, and bringing along the attitude that we need not explain or offer commentary on the objects we choose, we draft a poem about the places we live, the things we value on our home ground, and the ideas that those things might carry forward to our readers.

Published Works Cited:

"Where I Live," Billy Collins, *Sailing Alone Around the Room* (New York, NY: Random House), 2001.

"Why I Live Here," Robert Cording, *Walking with Ruskin* (Fort Lee, NJ: CavanKerry Press), 2010.

"Framing the Morning," Jack Ridl, *Broken Symmetry* (Detroit, MI: Wayne State University Press), 2006.

Other Worlds, in Other Words

by

Robert Wrigley

It is desperately easy for young poets to fall in love with the sound of their own voices, with their own words. Allen Ginsberg might have quipped "first word, best word," but the revisions of "Howl" suggest that he did not believe it. The lesson this assignment means to offer is simply this: there are many ways to say a thing and not all of them are equal. Or, that rewriting that which doesn't seem to need rewriting is a way of arriving at somewhere surprising, and often superior.

Re-writing for the purposes of developing an alternative to even the most seemingly ordinary of declarations is not only part of the revision process, it is part of all writing. It is an essential element in the shaping of a poem, and if we, as we write, are sometimes blind to other possibilities, here is a way to be stimulated into other ways of seeing and saying.

The assignment:

1. Write a brief, free verse poem, no shorter than ten lines, no longer than fourteen. Once the poem has arrived at a presentable, class-worthy draft, enter it into an on-line foreign language.

2. All original English versions of the poem, as well as the translation, should be turned into the instructor. A second translated version of the poem should be shuffled around the class, until at a signal from the instructor the shuffling stops.

3. Each student is then faced with a poem in a foreign language (without the name of the poet on it; anonymity is very important in this process) that he/she must translate from that tongue back into English.

Experts tell us that *Google Translate* has roughly the linguistic sophistication of a ten- year-old—someone, in other words, with imagination to spare but not a lot of syntactical or lexical or idiomatic skills. Therefore the version that emerges from GT will be somewhere between different and astonishingly mangled.

4. Make of the assisted translation the best poem you can, maintaining as much fidelity as you can to what seems to be the poem's intent.

For example, here is an anonymous poem of twelve lines:

Bean

Lichen, moss, and mouse fur, a nest
vastly out of proportion to what was
nurtured in it, it fills a five-gallon bucket

and must have been here for months,
since it's deep in the ten stacks of cordwood
in the woodshed, and late March, when I find it.

Soft as the hair of child, and as light.
And here's a pinkish, desiccated mousling
the size of a great northern bean:

eyelash feet, a tail-stub that breaks off
in my palm, and two pin-prick eye holes,
in which a tiny oblivion beckons.

Now here is the same poem, translated (via GT) into Italian:

Fagiolo

Licheni, muschi e mouse pelliccia, un nido

notevolmente sproporzionato rispetto a ciò che era
nutrita in esso, si riempie un cinque-gallone secchio

e deve essere stata qui per mesi,
dal momento che è profondo nei dieci pile di legna da
    ardere
nella legnaia, e la fine di marzo, quando lo trovo.

Morbidi come i capelli del bambino, e come la luce.
Ed ecco un rosato, mousling essiccato le
dimensioni di un chicco grande nord:

piedi di ciglia, una coda-stub che interrompe
nel palmo della mia mano, e due pin-prick fori per gli
    occhi,
in cui un piccolo chiama oblio.

Now here is the same poem, translated back into English (also via GT):

Bean

Lichens, mosses and mouse fur, a nest
greatly disproportionate to what was
fed into it, fills a five-gallon bucket

and must have been here for months,

since it is deep in the ten stacks of firewood
in the woodshed, and the end of March, when I find
    him.

Soft like baby hair, and how the light.
And here is a rose, dried mousling
the size of a grain far north:

feet of an eye, a tail-stub that interrupts
in the palm of my hand, and two pin-prick holes for the
    eyes,
calls in which a small oblivion.

The differences in the two English versions man-
age to be both slight and enormous. What seems fairly
well-made gets twisted a little syntactically, and the diction
shifts a register or two. The unidiomatic phrasings will
have to be retooled and made clear, and the poem that
results may, or may not, be something like the same poem.

The fun—the instructive fun—comes in, at last,
the comparing of the two English versions. In the old
party game, the one in which a joke is passed around a
room, the joke usually gets much if not all of the humor
bled out of it. Not so with this assignment. Sometimes
the translation comes out far more interesting. The
question to ask, in such an event, is how, and why?

Conjuring Place in Poetry

by

Sheryl St. Germain

Too often the study of place is relegated to prose; we teach students of fiction and nonfiction how to evoke a strong sense of place in narrative, but rarely do we teach poets the value of deep attention to a physical place. These exercises will help students explore the intelligence of places, both natural and cultivated, and will give them tools to write about the profound, conflicting, and sometimes unwanted ways that place enters, shapes, and even transforms us. Birthplace, wilderness, suburbia, cityscape—whether gloriously wild, fulsomely peopled, or ruinously barren, any place that's been important to us can fuel the engine of a poem.

Mapmaking

Have the students make a visual map of a place that is important to them. It could be a map of their childhood or current neighborhood, a park, a vacation spot, or a city or town that holds strong memories for them. It could be a place to which they are innately and intensely drawn, or a place that holds strong memories, either pleasant or disturbing ones. The geographical details should be as correct as they can get them, but it's just as important that they map emotional details.

It may, in fact, be more important to map the exact location in their backyard where they experienced their first kiss, for example, or buried their dog, than to get the exact elevation of the landscape. What activity do they associate with this place? Is there a smell, a food, a culture they associate with this place? What kind of trees grow in their neighborhoods and cities, what kind of bodies of water might dominate the landscape?

After they've made the map, have them write a draft of a poem that follows the map in whatever way seems important to them. They may not want to include all the details of the map in the draft; maybe the simple act of making the map has reminded them about how much they loved picking blackberries with their brother in the fields behind the family home, for example, or of the importance of bodies of water, farms, hills or levees, to their sense of self.

Students of all ages up through my MFA students usually enjoy this exercise, and sometimes make very elaborate maps on large sheets of paper that they then share with the class. Just the physical act of drawing the map reminds them of many things they thought they had forgotten, and sometimes they are able to generate several poems from one map. I like the exercise because it genuinely privileges place: it forces us to see how closely linked with place our memories are, to see that place is not merely a "setting" for our memories, but in some cases the container and inspiration for the memory.

Here is an excerpt from a long poem I wrote titled "Going Home" about my birth city, New Orleans, using the map exercise to generate an initial draft:

It's all there in the disappearing light:
all the evenings of slow sky and slow loving, slow
    boats on
sluggish bayous;
the thick-middled trees with the slow-sounding
    names—
oak, mimosa, pecan, magnolia;

the slow tree sap that sticks in your hair when you lie with
the trees;
and the maple syrup and pancakes and grits, the butter
melting slowly
into and down the sides like sweat between breasts of
sloeeyed strippers;
and the slow-throated blues that floats over the city
like fog;
and the weeping, the willows, the cut onions, the
cayenne,
the slow-cooking beans with marrow-thick gravy;
and all the mint juleps drunk so slowly on all the slow
southern porches,
the bourbon and sugar and mint going down warm and
brown, syrup and slow;
and all the ice cubes melting in all the iced teas,
all the slow-faced people sitting
in all the slowly rocking rockers...

This poem doesn't function as a map in that you
won't learn where the trees with the thick middles are,
or the sluggish bayous, or the slow southern porches;
the poem is rather an emotional map that resonates,
I would hope, because of the deep attention to the
strong markers of place. Those markers evoke a sense

of slow movement; in this case, like that of the Mississippi, the river inside which the poem nests.

Metaphor-making

This next exercise easily grows out of the map-making exercise, taking it one step further. Have the students focus on one element of a landscape they have mapped—it could be a tree, a body of water, a plant, an animal, or a landform that is rich enough to suggest a natural symbol for something else.

Sometimes the best way to do this is to suggest they focus on something they're drawn to for reasons they don't understand, then allow themselves the freedom to explore all avenues for the attraction. For example, a polluted lake or the multi-seeded pomegranate might suggest something about the nature of family; a spawning salmon's desire to get back to its birth waters may remind one of our own desire to go home again. The rendering of the body of water, land, flora, or fauna should serve as a metaphor for something larger.

Here is a short poem, "The Lake," in which I focused my attention on a lake of my childhood, Lake Pontchartrain:

I think it was always polluted,
even as a child I remember that gray peppered foam

mouthing the shore. Some days it had a rotten smell to it,
especially hot days when the fish that had tried so hard
to filter the shit through their gills gave up
and floated open-eyed to the surface.
I used to be amazed at what could thrive in that lake,
scavengers, shellfish, how white and sweet their meat was.
Its name was French like mine: Pontchartrain,
St. Germain, and the names echo each other nights
when I feel those waters rising, and the dead fish all
      rise up,
the dark waters swelling higher and higher
until I have to give it up or drown,
swim for whatever hard-shelled goodness I can find.

In the case of this poem, making the map helped
me to acknowledge, in a more visceral way, that I had
grown up between two influential bodies of water,
Lake Pontchartrain and the Mississippi River. Moving
on to this next exercise, I remembered how much time
I had spent at the lake, which was only a few blocks
from my house, and in focusing my attention on the
lake I was able to remember the astonishment I felt
as a young girl looking at the crabs that performed a
kind of alchemy I would hope for later in the poems
I would write as an adult. The details of what I saw

when I looked into the waters of the lake led to an insight about the creative process for me.

These exercises encourage students to consider place as a valuable tool and muse for the writing of poems, one to which they can return repeatedly.

Published Works Cited:

"Going Home," Sheryl St. Germain, *Let it Be a Dark Roux: New and Selected Poems* (Pittsburgh, PA: Autumn House Press, 2007)

"The Lake," Sheryl St. Germain, *Let it Be a Dark Roux: New and Selected Poems* (Pittsburgh, PA: Autumn House Press, 2007)

The Poet as Field Researcher

by

Charlotte Pence

"In every writer, there is a certain amount of the scavenger," William Faulkner wrote. Writers often recognize a part of themselves as scavengers, whether by reusing a line of dialogue overhead on the bus or recreating the scent from peeling an orange.

Our sense of scavenging today is to salvage what someone else disposes, but according to the OED, a *scavenger* originally meant a person employed to clean streets or a church.

It's this initial denotation of cleansing—to remove the grime from public objects and place them back in the public sphere—that I use to help students learn the distinction between showing and telling.

During a recent workshop, the class came to a poem filled with statements such as "she sits on the park bench / sad and lonely." "But how can we see this?" I prodded. "What details are communicating sadness to us?" "You just can tell," the student writer replied. His mind was so rapidly processing visual cues, he couldn't articulate what exactly revealed to him the person's emotional state. To help my students slow down and articulate the details that bring about a particular experience in a poem, I created an exercise based on the procedures of field researchers such as anthropologists and ethnographers.

First, I ask students to choose a "culture" whose use of language or rituals interest them. Focusing on a culture helps students think about themselves as researchers. We sometimes need to brainstorm on types of cultures and how that term can be considered very loosely to include hockey fans, Baptist preachers, or college classrooms so that students begin to see all the opportunities. Some places where my students visited with the most success included a punk concert, a comic book store/gaming center, and even a poetry slam.

Places that didn't work as well were places that students tended to visit anyway, such as a club meeting at which they were already members. The key is for the student to feel like an outsider, and yet be comfortable enough to quietly observe from a distance. For example, one student hated the culture of football at the University of Tennessee, so she attended a game. Her notes yielded fresh details partly because she noticed what a typical football fan might have grown used to such as the acceptance of littering or how many people leave before the game is over.

Once students determine their sites, I explain how ethnographers typically conduct research by taking field notes, which includes not only listing dialogue, but also detailing the setting and their reactions. I then ask the students to draw a line down the middle of the page and write "Observations" on one side and "Reactions" on the other. This simple task is key. It helps young writers separate details that will "show" from statements that will "tell." Once all of this is discussed, I tell them to get out there in the field and get to work, bringing back twenty or so observations from their research.

When they return to the classroom, I ask students to re-read the field notes and highlight seven details that stand out because of their vividness, their complexity, or their strangeness. Then, I give the writing assignment: write a poem, no more than twenty lines, that includes four details from their field notes and that withholds giving a reaction until the end of the poem. Not only do the field notes help the poems deliver some good details, but the notes remind students of the difference between showing and telling. Abstract language that might have crept in before is now more readily understood to be a reaction—or telling—because of that line down the middle of the notes.

One set of field notes that resulted in an effective poem was written by Heather Campbell. She attended a worship service and included some of the pastor's sermon as well as details from the communion to shape her poem. Here is the beginning of her poem "Modern Disciple":

> sitting in the sanctuary of hope church, 9 a.m.,
> Pastor Chris stands behind a lace covered table,
> a broken loaf of Bread
> on a blue glazed plate, tiny
> plastic cylinders filled with
> Mott's Grape Juice.
> The pastor speaks,
> *will you come?*
>
> I carry my half awake body to
> the Bread of Life, tear
> a chunk of soft center and shove it in
> my mouth.

I was pleased by how she pulled back from giving her reaction to the communion, but instead chose details that cue the reader in to her skepticism: the inclusion of the name brand, Mott's, diminishes the sense of holiness; the verb "shoves" gives a slapdash impression as does "tearing" a "chunk" of the bread. Nothing in the writing signals a high sense of deference from the speaker. The poem ends with the pastor "dismissing" the congregation, and the poet uses this phrasing to indicate her sense of spiritual failure.

> *amen. you are all dismissed.*

> I pull my arms through the sleeves
> of my leather jacket, peer at
> the table laced in Life, I turn away,
> through the door, spewed out.

While the assignment allows for a reaction in the last line, the poem uses word choice, action, the title, and the epigraph to convey her point. The epigraph is from Revelations 3:16 and states: "So then because you are lukewarm, and neither cold nor hot, I will spew you out of my mouth." Because of the assignment's emphasis on separating observation from reaction, the poem discovers multiple ways to communicate its meaning. In the end, the poet trusts that details and word choice, especially echoing "spew" at the end, are more than enough to convey her point.

Another student's observation site was the university library. As I mentioned earlier, sometimes well-known locations do not yield great results, but this student fully embraced his role of researcher and approached the library as if it were a foreign country. He spent two hours in the library with a tape recorder, notebook, and maps, easily blending in and "spying" on the students.

He happened upon a couple kissing among the stacks and another student hiding notes in books, but what he focused on was something a bit more ordinary: an overheard cell phone conversation. Apparently, a student was fighting with his mother over the phone, whining about needing more money. This call reminded the student of his own relationship with his mother. So, he called to thank her for all that she did for him. That call ended up turning into another fight—all of which the student recorded.

His poem focused on his own phone call, but because he had approached the call as a researcher and recorded it, he was able to create a complex poem that revealed interesting character flaws. "I just wanted to say thanks," is repeated but turns from pleasant to sarcastic in tone as the mother asks, "Why are you saying this now?" Both mother and speaker reveal communication problems, and it is exactly that fact that becomes so refreshing. Few beginning poems present the speaker as culpable, but this poem did partly because the poet owned his role as researcher who was wedded to the facts.

On the other hand, one student's field notes were rich with details, but the final poem lacked a point. This student chose to write about rural culture and visited his grandparent's farm in Carthage, Tennessee. The day he visited, his grandmother was canning bread and butter pickles, so his observations centered on the kitchen. They included counters sticky with sugar syrup, air moist from the boiling water, and plastic pink wall tiles streaked with grease. His reactions tended toward the positive and talked about how he loved his grandmother or about how he looked forward to eating the pickles. In the end, his poem lacked a conflict, so the details didn't ever quite add up. Still, entering the field as a researcher will inform his future writing process.

I also have found it helpful to read some poems that do exactly what the assignment is asking for so that an analysis of "show, don't tell" can occur. Some of my favorites include "Eating Alone" by Li-Young Lee, "In the Memphis Airport" by Timothy Steele, and

"Lying in a Hammock at William Duffy's Farm in Pine Island, Minnesota" by James Wright.

Wright's poem is one I love to teach because the final line of "I have wasted my life" is shocking on first read. "Where did *that* come from?" they often wonder. This last line, I remind them, synthesizes what all the details have been working to communicate. So, if we reduced Wright's poem to fit our assignment, his synthesis is one of awe, and his four observations about the butterfly, the cowbells, the horse droppings, and the chicken hawk, all led to this reaction in the last line.

Seeing as how the last line can be read positively or negatively, I have students track with a positive (+), negative (-), or neutral sign (/), how each detail makes them feel. Then, I have them tally these. What is predominant for them? With interpretations of the last line ranging from a negative sense of uselessness to a powerful sense of perspective, the tallies can help one understand why they interpret the line as they do. By discussing the subtleties of the poem's observations, the class sees how detail is not the goal; rather, the precise detail that leads to the synthesis is the goal.

The influence of ethnographic field notes helps young writers begin to separate their reactions from their observations, which is key to understanding when to show and when to tell. This type of ethnographic approach moves the student from happening upon a good detail to consciously entering the world as a writer and scavenger who cleans what others have left in the dust.

Tunneling through the Dark

by

Megan Grumbling

When I agreed to act as poet mentor to a city
police officer, I had an inkling that here would be no
place for any elevated academic chatter. These suspicions were confirmed once my partner, the whip-smart
young Detective Kelly Gorham, hit me with the sce-
nario of her first poem:

*Out on a late-night call, early in my career, I pull up
in a cruiser and scope out an abandoned lot: voices shouting, a
crowd gathering, parked cars in the way of my sight lines, lots
of people in the shadows. I shine my flashlight into the dark and
identify the suspect – though I can't see him too well – and raise
my weapon. He seems to be aiming something at me – something
shiny – but I can't make out what. So I have one split-second
to decide whether or not to fire on the guy. And I'm a heartbeat
away from shooting; I'm this close. But I don't. Then, just an*

instant later, I see what the shiny thing actually is – a silver cast on the guy's broken arm. Not a gun at all.

Talk about immediacy, vital details, and decision-making! We writers are always spouting about these things, but here was a real-life situation in which Kelly was forced to focus on only the most crucial, life-or-death essentials of the scene, and to make a choice. She was a natural when we took much the same approach to honing her poem. It's this strategy that I suggest for teachers working with new poets who are most comfortable with their own narratives: ask students to arrive at their scenes – just as Kelly had to – prepared to filter out all the background distractions and deal with the essentials of their stories.

Kelly was new to poetry, but she fearlessly took on the crash-course demanded by "Thin Blue Lines," a program in Portland, Maine that paired poets with officers to help them write about their experiences on the force. The project would conclude—a mere three weeks later!—with the poems' publication in a calendar to be sold as a benefit for the family of a recently deceased officer. A worthy endeavor, and we got right to it:

1. I asked her to start by free writing in a straight-up narrative voice, to simply sketch out her harrowing

encounter with power and darkness. She wrote up a promising beginning, and then we came to what was, for her, the less familiar part of the poetry-writing process: the poetry part.

I talked about how poetry's difference from prose is that poetry "distills" what we would normally say and how we say it. How, like whisky, it's strong and comes in small doses. How often, in poetry, "things are more than what they are." That is to say, I explained, the things in poems are, of course, just things, but they often also stand for something bigger than themselves—a time, a truth, a hurt.

2. We then discussed the images she had used in her narrative as if they were clues or leads. Kelly's grasp of this idea was quick and intuitive, which shouldn't have surprised me—after all, her career as a detective had trained her to make vital decisions based on small details that suggest a larger situation. We talked about how she'd done this in her own work: sizing up a suspect and his intentions by a certain answer to her question, or by a certain grin a little too askew. In a very real way, she understood symbol and metaphor a lot more viscerally, and more practically, than I did.

3. I then asked her to go back to her free-write. First, she was to distill the stories to their basics (how

gratifying, the fun she had crossing out the fatty details and liberating phrases from articles!). Then, she would identify which elements from her first draft might be candidates for "things that are more than what they are." Here's some of what she found:

Her flashlight, shining into that dim place but not lighting much up, was not just a flashlight: it could also be seen as her limited ability to figure out what was happening out there in the chaos. She also saw significance in her hands juggling both a flashlight and a gun, two very different tools. The cast, too, was obviously more than just a cast, but also a symbol of a potentially huge mistake of perception. And the word "see" had a lot going on with it, she said, because what she first "sees" isn't what's really there at all – and what hangs on the question is no small matter. Later on in the poem, "seeing" comes to mean more than just visually making out the cast, but also understanding the enormity of what she'd been close to doing.

Not only was Kelly spot-on in finding these pressure points in her piece, but talking about them seemed to give her an even stronger sense of her story's larger implications. This wasn't just one crazy anecdote from the street beat, after all, but had served to truly shake her up, as a reminder of the constant dangers of her profession and her power. Going deeper into finding the "things that are more than what they are" helped to her grasp the full fright of her tale.

4. So we came then to the question of what to do with these crucial things that are more than they are, once we've rooted them out. Since these are the pressure points of the poem, I suggested, they're good places to press on a little harder – to give a little more tension, more weight, more pang – and there are some easy ways poets can do this:

a. First, we might simply call on the five senses to describe one of these important elements in more detail, lingering on it a little (though always remembering to distill!), and putting the reader even more in our skin.

b. We might also use one of these pressure points in deciding where to end lines (often a particular point of uncertainty for new poets): Ending a line mid-phrase throws a lot of attention onto that last word, makes the reader hold her breath for a second, and can set the word up for double meanings and other fun stuff.

c. Finally, we might repeat a key element at different points in the poem, possibly in such a way that by the final line, the meaning of the word or phrase has changed.

Over two weeks of work and discussions, Kelly worked with these three basic tools to help emphasize the key elements of her poem that she'd identified, and in the process she also identified a few others: in thinking about what might want more close details, she realized that the actual sensation of her hand on her weapon was important for the reader to feel. So she elaborated with some description:

> Finger on the trigger. Tension like a circus wire.
> Grip tight. Pain shoots through my hand.

As for working with the end-line, Kelly used enjambment nicely to get across the stirring dual meaning of "see." She'd already used the verb mid-line throughout the poem, so the way she ends the line with it here is striking; it prolongs the suspense and gives the moment the extra weight of an initiation:

> He tries to follow orders.
>
> Prones out, watching.
>
> That's when I see
>
> for the first time:
>
> Broad. Solid. Camouflaging his arm.

Finally, it was in using refrain that Kelly truly nailed her poem: The phrase "Man with a gun" appears early on, as if it were simply the complaint she was responding to, and it repeats verbatim shortly thereafter, in description of what she believes she sees, or as it might repeat in her racing mind. But the phrase changes in the final lines of her poem, to dramatic effect:

> Man with a broken arm.
>
> Man without
>
> a gun.
>
> Only a silver cast.

By the end of our three weeks, Kelly had titled the poem "Tunnel Vision," and it was chosen as a featured poem for the calendar (it headlined February):

Tunnel Vision

Pushing a cruiser on late out.

Man with a gun.

Sweat on my brow. Pulse races.

I jump out of the cruiser. They've been shot, a voice screams. Cross

the sidewalk.

Crowd forming. Gun ready. Flashlight shining into darkness.

I see him. Man with a gun.

Show me your hands. Drop the gun. Get on the ground.

What I saw was silver, shiny and it pointed at my head.

I see a gun.

Finger on the trigger. Tension like a circus wire.

Grip tight. Pain shoots through my hand.

Raises hands to my commands, my flashlight catches silver.

A millisecond and he'd be gone. But the silver?

He tries to follow orders.

Prones out, watching.

That's when I see

for the first time:

Broad. Solid. Camouflaging his arm.

Man with a broken arm.

Man without

a gun.

Only a silver cast.

From Kelly's work out in the thick of very real hazard and hurt, she brought to our process not just fraught subjects to appraise, but also an urgency and need for precision that I think poets can learn from. By adopting Kelly's m.o. toward their own work, students can practice economy and intensity, and can become more forceful and decisive in their own narrative verse. Starting the exercise as a group can grease the wheel:

1. Show the class a scene – a still photograph of a crowd or busy street, or some other image in which there's a lot going on. Give them a very short amount of time on their own to size up this scene, to determine one key event that's taking center stage, and to decide what is essential – only the barest, most vital necessities of clues and glints – in telling the story.

Students will likely see a range of different things going on in the image, and this will make for interesting discussion. Why are each student's chosen details important specifically to the scene he or she sees taking place? How are these elements bigger than what they are?

2. Then ask students to draft a short poem, sketching the scene's story around the details they've chosen.

3. Have them then return to their draft and work with one poet's tool to send home the significance of

those details – I suggest refrain, for its simplicity and for the movement and cohesion it can bring to a narrative.

4. Finally, ask them to repeat the whole process, this time writing from their own memory, their own stories.

Once Kelly and I had finished writing together and her poems had rolled off the press, I was left with a new appreciation for the subtlety and difficulty of her own calling, as well as for what her work has in common with poets' work: the need to make wholes of parts, to decipher glints in the dim. I was also struck by how powerfully and practically poetry can serve the daily, messy, thorny world in which we live.

As a poet, though, I'm often as guilty as the next gal of holing up in my writing room and getting cerebral. And as a teacher, I know how hard it can be to keep a classroom discussion from spiraling into abstractions. But working with Kelly in our unconventional partnership reminded me of what all we poets know: That our best and most necessary work happens when we take ourselves out of the safe rooms and into the world. With the perspective we gain out there, we can encourage our students to engage the common, precarious world in their own work, and to arrive on their own difficult scenes with courage, even in the face of danger and the dark.

Assigning the Elegy

by

Claudia Emerson

    I have taught undergraduates for most of my teaching career, and particularly in introductory workshops, I have handed out an assignment for every poem. I learned early on that if I didn't give the students a great deal of guidance at the outset, we all wasted a lot of time with early uninformed drafts filled with abstraction and an overabundance of the lyric "I" from those who had worked on their high school literary magazines, or the opposite but equally frustrating problem of drafts from the diligent English major who had not read anything more modern than Milton. The workshop exists and succeeds because it saves all of us time in our writing lives, so the more I can do to move us all toward productive, varied discussion, the better.

While I assign poems in any number of various meters and forms in upper level workshops, I also simply recommend kinds of poems to the students—anything from epistle to persona to apostrophe. One assignment with which I have had a great deal of success is the elegy. I wasn't sure at first that the assignment would generate much excitement. Again, these are undergraduates, some late adolescents, but mostly young adults—mostly healthy and unencumbered. What about elegy might excite them?

But at the time, I was writing a lot of poems in this custom—or poems elegiac in tone—so I gave out of fairly bare-bones assignment sheet:

> For your poem, you will write an **elegy** (from Gr. *Elegeia*, "lament"). According to the *Princeton Encyclopedia of Poetry and Poetics*, the **elegy** is a "lyric, usually formal in tone and diction, suggested either by the death of an actual person or by the poet's contemplation of the tragic aspects of life." The **lyric**, according to Thrall's *A Handbook to Literature*, is a "brief subjective poem marked by imagination, melody, and emotion, and creating a single, unified impression."

Class discussions centered on the elegy as not necessarily morbid but also as celebration of the something lost; we talked about taking liberally the notion of elegy and considered lament as well within the parameters of the genre. I brought in several examples of elegy from a wonderful anthology entitled *Inventions of Farewell* edited by Sandra M. Gilbert, poems that demonstrated the wide range of possibilities. Among favorites with the students over time: Betty Adcock's "Poem for Dizzy," Yusef Komunyakaa's "Facing It," Richard Wilbur's "The Pardon," Elizabeth Bishop's "First Death in Nova Scotia," and Gregory Orr's "Gathering the Bones Together."

We also discussed being broad-minded about the definition of lyric. Lyric also may imply a narrative—but doesn't give the whole story. The emphasis is then on image and emotion, on metaphor, and not "what happened."

I made sure that some formal guidelines were part of this assignment. While I allow students' verse to be "free," I have long felt ethically bound to make certain that undergraduates, mostly English majors, understand that mastering standard punctuation isn't something poets are immediately liberated from in a creative writing classroom. Thus, my guidelines were all created to have young poets begin to understand the beautiful tensions that arise from sentences "turning" into lines in a poem—and the ways lines have their own integrity within and apart from the sentence. (Since a few of my literature colleagues abhor close reading, my students may never have thought about these aspects of any poet's writing process.)

Format:

Properly punctuated and adhere to other conventions of written English such as normal capitalization.

At least fifteen lines long:

    no line with fewer than seven syllables.

    no line with more than fifteen syllables.

    at least four enjambed lines.

    Times New Roman or Courier, flush left.

Consider:

Word choice.

Sound.

Concrete images, significant detail.

Line integrity.

Figures of speech: metaphor, simile.

Tone.

Poetry is for me the highest ordering of language, so while I realize that my "rules" seem pretty strict on reading them, I have always spent a lot of time talking about moving from idea/conceit to form, and students have learned quickly from the format guidelines that there are many, many choices the free verse poet makes when employing the line.

They understood from the beginning that I didn't mean for them to begin writing with a syllable count in mind—and I have also put the following quote from Ralph Waldo Emerson at the top of the assignment as a reminder: "The thought and the form are equal in the order of time, but in the order of genesis the thought is prior to the form." Still, the line length I recommend falls somewhere around the pentameter line, which, to me, has always been the optimum length for the eye and ear to take in.

Besides confusing elegy with eulogy in a few cases, the students did and have continued to respond well to the prompt and with pretty amazing results. My students, despite all the liberties and possibilities of their youth, live very complicated lives in an increasingly complicated world, and the elegy brings with it the burden, perhaps, to look to the personal—but not necessarily to the private. They tend to take the assignment seriously, and they write poems they actually care about. The elegy is not the place where theoretical, intellectual or literary fashion rules; instead, the elegy prompt makes them write about something—some-one, a place, a time—with care.

The risks are obvious. The elegy can lean mightily toward sentimentality—but as Richard Hugo reminds us in *The Triggering Town* (paraphrasing his colleague Bill Kittredge), "if you are not *risking* sentimentality, you are not close to your inner self." In addition, we have talked a lot in workshop about clichés in terms of language and figures—as well as clichéd ways of expressing emotion.

Still, we know that grief, profound sorrow, regret, and despair are not clichés—but rather shared emotions that are part of the landscape of any life not matter how well spent. As you might expect, I have read elegies about the deaths of a parent or grandparent, but I have also read elegies for their parents' failed marriages, a house lost in a divorce, innocence in the process.

Some students have also written very much to the side of traditional elegy. One student wrote, for example, about seeing an orangutan on display in a zoo; the speaker thinks of how the animal would behave in its natural habit, closing the poem with the epiphany that orangutans are "the most solitary primate. / I'm still for a moment. / We understand." The elegiac impulse of the poem is on the self as much as on the animal—the mourning not only of freedom but of solitude. In a similar mindset, another student wrote about visiting an aquarium where children "tap on the glass and stare" to no avail, the fish looking "sideways in that fish / way, chanting quietly with your fins, I will swim / or die. I will swim or die." Again, the lament here is far more for the humans who have designed such a place—and not so much for the fish who resist some part of the captivity by ignoring the tapping captors.

With elegy, this assignment, and the various responses to it in mind, I have begun recently to write and talk with my students about poems' various architectures—and elegy in particular—as having many variations on what I call the "poetics of threshold." While poems have long been considered to "turn," they might sometimes be better described as having places where the reader (and the writer for that matter) must cross over to another place in the poem, sometimes to remain—but often to go back out the way they came, but changed by the *passage*, a beautifully complex word denoting moving through time, space, and text.

Threshold is a psychological term as well, dealing with perception of feeling and discernible change in feeling; we all use the idea of threshold with pain, and that seems appropriate to the consideration of the experiences and impulses that lead us to poetry—and to elegy in particular. The threshold is the strongest, one of the most defining places in the house, but it is also the place where no one can stay.

The crossing of an emotional threshold by writing into and past strong emotion changes the writer first, and Gregory Orr in *Poetry as Survival* and Judith Harris in *Signifying Pain* have guided my thinking about the creative distancing that helps make trauma "other"—a helpful thing to the poet writing out of great pain—and then renders the experience into an art form that may then allow readers into places they have never been, but have nevertheless known intimately.

I continue to love the opportunities for teaching about poetry at its gut level importance, engaging young poets in writing that introduces them to poetry's lasting power. And part of that power is what poetry teaches the writer about the self—through the disciplined act of creating something *outside* the self, through the distancing that comes with ordering the chaos of emotion.

Witness, Testimony, and Fact

by

Laurie Lamon

"Last Pure Dusky Seaside Sparrow Dies." I read this small headline many years ago and was moved by the quiet tragedy of this singular fact. The headline has stayed with me as an equally resonating poetic line, a beautiful example of found poetry.

I've used this headline as a way to introduce a "Poem of Witness" assignment for my upper-division students. I ask them to consider it both as a fact of science and as a line of poetry. I want them to consider the simplicity, the emotional effect, the formal tone created by the stressed monosyllables and the trochaic meter of the three polysyllables, the alliteration of "Dusky" and "Dies," and the layering of consonant sounds in the final four words. The sentence is a rich, slow experience of language. Each of the four particular details is necessary in telling a particular reality.

"To witness" means to furnish proof, to tell personal knowledge of something, to have seen something. It means to "tell" (to count, to relate in detail, to make known). Some poems of witnesses tell for those who have been silenced or oppressed. Carolyn Forche's "The Colonel" is a famous example. The work of these poems isn't to tell us what we already know: that oppression is wrong and dictators are evil. Forche's poem tells us that dictators have homes, pets, dining-room tables. They are husbands and fathers. The most terrifying detail for me is not the sack of human ears the colonel spills before the Americans as proof of his power. It is horrifying, but not unexpected. What is more chilling is the fact that in this home a pistol is not out of place on a sofa cushion.

In addition to "The Colonel," I provide a packet of "witness" examples that includes Robert Haas's "A Story About the Body," Philip Larkin's "Born Yesterday" and "Water," Jane Kenyon's "While We Were Arguing," Adrienne Rich's "Like This Together," Yahuda Amichai's "Near the Wall of a House," Jack Gilbert's "Going Wrong," and "Singapore" by Mary Oliver.

I know my students have not experienced the historical enormities of anxiety and suffering that poets such as Forche, Amichai, Janos Pilinszky, and Dahlia Ravikovitch, to name a few, have witnessed or lived through. However, they have experienced family love, and family ruptures, the illnesses of grandparents and parents. Some have learned the vocabulary of cancer and Alzheimer's. Many have traveled extensively; many have worked meaningfully in underprivileged communities. They live with the internet's seemingly limitless means of affecting their experience of community, music, language, and even time itself. It is to these subjects as well I suggest they turn with this assignment:

Background:

1. Consider and take notes about what occupies your time, what comprises the images that surround you. What does your soul invite and what does it reject?

2. Read newspaper and magazine articles on issues and topics that you care about. Take notes on how images and uses of language affect you.

3 Consider when you have ever stepped outside of yourself and felt the reality of another.

Writing:

1. Establish a particular voice. Who is speaking? Who should be speaking, given your subject?

2. Focus on particulars and avoid abstractions (the best description of hunger is described as a loaf of bread; pain as divorce papers; love as the white sheet on the hospital bed).

3. Don't be afraid to repeat key words and syllables, in order to build a pattern of sounds. Listen to your vowels and consonants as we hear them in that newspaper headline, "Last Pure Dusky Seaside Sparrow Dies."

4. Limit your poem to thirty lines, and title your poem *after* you have you have "finished" it— that is, discover your title in the writing process.

I also include Amichai's poem "Try to Remember Some Details" on the assignment hand-out because it works so well in getting the students to think particularly about the use of voice, form, and specific diction. Here's the first stanza:

Try to remember some details. Remember the clothing
    of the one you love

so that on the day of disaster you'll be able to say: last
    seen
wearing such-and-such, brown jacket, white hat.
Try to remember some details. For they have no face
and their soul is hidden and their crying
is the same as their laughter,
and their silence and their shouting rise to one height
and their body temperature is between 98 and 104
    degrees
and they have no life outside this narrow space
and they have no graven image, no likeness, no mem-
    ory
and they have paper cups on the day of their rejoicing
and disposable paper plates.

    The voice is controlled, instructive, authoritative.
The speaker has experienced "the day of disaster" and is
arming the reader, who has not lived such a day, with the
tools of recovery. Our memory of the living must outlive
disaster, memory which is confronted with the "such-
and-such" of a beloved's clothing which has become
artifact, and by the end of the stanza, less than that: fragile, impermanent, disposable. The poem uses repetition,
catalogue, paradox (all those "and's" and" no's), and the
particularized images of precious ordinariness, "brown
jacket, white hat." How is it to be endured, human life as

fragile as "disposable paper plates? "Try to Remember Some Details" is also an elegy for "all of them" that "the earth will swallow," and the "all" of us who follow from our own lives of curses and blessings.

Finally, there are natural pitfalls to this assignment. A poem is not a tract, an editorial, or a judgment. The poem that aims for shock value will be interesting only once, if then. While I've read my share of the inauthentic poem, the usurped-experienced poem, the dogmatic poem, that's ok. More often than not, I have been astounded by the control and beauty of the work these "inexperienced" witnesses bring to the table.

To conclude, here are two poems by writers whose voices, clear and authentic, and whose diction, remarkable in its tact and control, avoid commenting rhetorically on historical injustice and cataclysm. Instead, they find the buried pulse, the living detail, the color, sound, and feel of innocence, and wakening awareness.

A Slow Process
by Haley Atkinson

On a road trip I listened to the memories
of a distant relative. She spoke of the small
cement shacks she remembers watching from

the backseat, as her family drove through town.
Small cement and brick boxes with thick blankets
and rugs covering the windows and the doors
heavy textiles, maroon and indigo
patterns flapping in the wind.

It would have been the spring of 1958,
the Little Rock Nine were attending Little Rock Central High
for the first time. Here, the children living in these
  homes
had darker skin, were taken on buses to schools far
  away from hers.

The photographs of the basketball teams, hanging
in the halls of my high school show the years in
the late 1970's students were bused
from schools farther north,
desegregation, a slow process.
At the end of one of these halls I sat with Jon.
In desks far too small for our long legs. We were to move
from small desk to small desk,
The Stations of the French Revolution, the board read.
The other partners waited, impatient, as I listened to Jon
stumble over the sounds

m - on - ar - ch — y

a - ris - to - cra - cy

ex - ecu - tion.

9/15
by Lydia Buchanan

Four days after 9/11, a storm

felled the Bradford pear.

My neighborhood friends and I

used the fallen trunk and branches

as a fort in our game of war,

ducking under its labyrinth of limbs

flattening our faces

into the sweet Indian summer blossoms.

A wave of invisible finger bullets

swept through the branches

and leveled us to our knees

again.

My mother reprimanded us.

Violent games are inappropriate after a tragedy.

How can you pretend to kill each other?

So many dead.

We grew silent as she went back into the house.

My lips popped, *bam, bam*.

Softly, I pointed my index finger

at my friend as I crouched

in the fallen branches.

Published Works Cited:

"Try to Remember Some Details," Yehuda Amichai, *The Selected Poetry of Yehuda Amichai*, Chana Bloch and Stephen Mitchell, trans. (Berkeley, CA: University of California Press), 1996.

An Assignment for the End of the Semester

by

Betsy Sholl

Here's an assignment worth trying toward the end of the semester: writing a long poem, one between sixty and a hundred lines. Having practiced using varieties of syntax and diction, having worked with sonic devices and experimented with several forms, the students are ready to try putting these elements of craft together by working on a longer poem.

I organize this assignment by reserving the last three weeks of the term and dividing the class into thirds. Each week, one third will hand in a draft of their long poems for workshop, while the other two groups work on their long poems or on other revisions for their portfolio.

To prepare for this assignment we talk about what kind of subjects can carry a long poem. I encourage students to think about what kinds of obsessions have already surfaced in their work. We talk about the questions that intrigue them, and the kinds of experiences that continue to baffle them and have no simple interpretation; we talk about the way our understanding of an event can change over time. Maybe there's an historical issue they are interested in exploring, or a relationship that could bear multiple lenses. I remind them that Grace Paley once said she knew she had a story when she had two stories, and we talk about how setting two elements in tension with each other can lead to a third—or more. We talk about creating a voice that can sustain a long poem, about various rhetorical structures and formal strategies, including anaphora, recurring image patterns, the use of sections, or the mixing of verse and prose as in haibun. We talk about the difference between staying in the present and moving through different moments of time.

As to specific ways of developing a long poem, one option is to develop a rhetorical pattern that can carry a continuous voice as it engages with its subject matter. We might read passages from James Schuyler and Walt Whitman, as well as Nazim Hikmet's "Things I Didn't Know I Loved." For some students, Hikmet's loose anaphora, his use of the present moment as a touchstone from which he departs via memory or associative thought becomes a model they can follow and draw on. The continual departure and return to a "home base" allows them to control the material while also allowing for surprise and improvisation. One student set her speaker on a long bus ride, creating a complex persona for her speaker as the mind between ear buds, half conductor, half automaton, registering the mix of landscape, music, and personal angst.

Another strategy is the braided narrative. In poems like Brigit Kelly's "The White Pilgrim" or "All Wild Animals Were Once Called Deer," students can trace the various strands of images, and see how the recurring use of those images leads the poem into insights not conceivable at the beginning. In other words, they see the images as crucial to the movement of the poem, not decoration or elaboration for its own sake, but a serious journey. In this mode, one student wrote about her summer teaching in China, working with details of landscape, her students, and her relationship with a problematic friend. The result was a poem that literally used its entire process to arrive at unexpected material and insights into the student's sense of displacement, and into the beauty and strangeness of the world.

Still another option to explore is the use of a poetic sequence. This is often the choice of students who prefer to work with compact or with highly elusive forms. I tend to focus on poems like Roethke's "The Shape of Fire," or Robert Hass's "Dragonflies Mating," in which the sections vary widely, and move the poem in different directions, each section qualifying or expanding the one before. Another model for a poem in sections might be Robert Hayden's "Middle Passage," with its use of collage and historical material.

Students find various ways to define their sequences. Some move logically through seasons or landscapes. Others are more associative, following the thread of a theme or obsession, looking at it from different angles. One focused on her ongoing fascination with images from Pompeii, starting with the childhood book she carried wherever she went, going on to her adolescent study of archeology, and her adult recognition of some of the psychological elements involved in her obsession with one specific figure from the ruins. The poem became an impressive and vivid meditation on servitude and will, the fragility of history, youth and age.

For some students the long poem becomes an exercise in revision—re: envisioning an earlier poem that didn't fulfill itself. They may get in touch with the original impulse behind the poem and explore it further, or they may find the earlier draft missed entirely the greater possibilities of their vision, and try a whole new approach. One specific way of opening up this process is have students add at least one new line between every line already in the poem. Even if this process begins mechanically, students soon see places they can further develop, areas they can look at more closely. One young women took a rather unpromising love poem and developed it into a rich, complex examination of a relationship, playing with various images of brilliance—the diamond ring, of course, but also sunlight on water, starlight, animal eyes in the dark, the way headlights can blind an oncoming driver....

Other options for working with revision include having students try writing twenty or more lines beyond the poem's current end to see what they turn up. Sometimes trying this several different times for several different days is useful. If one extension doesn't work, the next may unearth new material. In this process, students can be encouraged to look for areas in their draft they might want to question, challenge, contradict or refute. They might consider a poem that includes second and third thoughts, so the end product traces the process of thought, the mind at work, considering and reconsidering its material. Often students have success in this mode, contrasting a "then and now" response to experience, sometimes working in chunks—"then," first, followed by "now"—sometimes alternating back and forth several times.

Interestingly, students understand almost immediately that to work with larger blocks or streams of material form is crucial. They know the goal isn't simply to meet the required number of lines, but rather to find a form that will carry them into a larger vision, a bigger poem than most of them will have written so far. That process seems to elicit a real commitment to exploration. If they hadn't already, they begin to see form as neither external nor accidental, but like a riverbank shaping and being shaped by its river. Even their first discarded attempts show them how form can expand or restrict their material. As they continue working, the very notion of length allows them to linger in the process and its possibilities.

I warn the class that the long poem may fail and leave them with only a fragment they want to pursue. But that's okay. The process of stretching themselves won't be for naught. In fact, the long poems almost always succeed—succeed because they enlarge the students' ambition and scope, stretch their technical skill, open up new stylistic possibilities, excite them about their work, and show them they can do more than they thought. One student, who had worked almost exclusively in a brief observations reminiscent of William Carlos Williams out drinking with Charles Bukowski, wrote a loose, long-lined poem about his father, structured by recurring images so rich in detail and feeling, humor and insight, when he finished reading the entire class applauded. The student himself had been so entrenched in his identity as a spare, imagist poet that it took him a while to appreciate his own achievement.

It is important to be flexible with this assignment, especially for students who are naturally prolix or who enjoy confounding their readers. Sometimes a student will need to try almost the opposite approach, to *cut* every other line in a poem, and then work with the new circuitry that's left. A student who delights in obscurity, to the consternation of readers, might be encouraged to think about the limits of complexity (what the human brain can actually absorb), and to work with short sections, honing his or her ability to achieve clarity. Experimental poets are sometimes happier if the assignment can involve the possibilities of a mongrel poem, drawing on both prose and verse, and various texts. A student who has severe resistance to length can be encouraged to write companion poems—a sort of poetic sequence with separate titles.

But I'm not sure I've ever had a student resist this assignment. By the end of the semester, students seem up to the challenge, and are not afraid of failing. If the assignment is challenging, it is also exhilarating. Longer poems often open up new territory in terms of subject and style, voice and technique. Students develop a larger vision, and a greater awareness of how form and content relate, how a poem can include second and third thoughts, and push beyond opening assumptions into surprising territory—an object lesson in the creative process.

CONTRIBUTORS

David Baker has been teaching for 35 years, including two years in public high schools, several as a graduate assistant, and has taught in the MFA programs at Ohio State and Michigan and the undergraduate program at Kenyon College. He is a regular faculty member, on rotation, with the MFA program for writers at Warren Wilson College, and holds the Thomas B. Fordham Chair of Poetry at Denison University where he's taught for twenty-seven years. David is the author or editor of fourteen books of poetry and criticism, mostly recently *Never-Ending Birds* (W.W. Norton) which was awarded the 2011 Theodore Roethke Memorial Poetry Prize.

Andrea Hollander (formerly Andrea Hollander Budy) is the author of four full-length poetry collections: *Landscape with Female Figure: New & Selected Poems 1982 - 2012* (Autumn House Press, 2013), *Woman in the Painting*

(Autumn House Press, 2006), *The Other Life* (Story Line Press, 2001), and *House Without a Dreamer* (Story Line Press, 1993), which won the Nicholas Roerich Poetry Prize. Other honors include the D. H. Lawrence Fellowship, a Pushcart Prize for memoir, the *Runes* Poetry Prize, the Subiaco Award for Excellence in the Writing and Teaching of Poetry, and two poetry fellowships from the National Endowment for the Arts. Frequently featured at writers' conferences and festivals throughout the United States, as well as in England and France, she splits her time between Portland, Oregon, and the Arkansas Ozarks, where since 1991 she has worked as the Writer-in-Residence at Lyon College, which awarded her the Lamar Williamson Prize for Excellence in Teaching.

Todd Davis has taught English and creative writing at the junior high, high school, undergraduate and graduate levels for the past 26 years. In that time he has won several teaching awards, including the Grace D. Long Award for Faculty Excellence in Teaching from Penn State University and the Jenefer M. Giannasi Award for Excellence in Teaching from Northern Illinois University. At present he teaches creative writing and environmental studies at Penn State University's Altoona College. He is the author of four books of poems, most recently *In the Kingdom of the Ditch* (Michigan State University Press, 2013) and *The Least of These* (Michigan

State University Press, 2010). He also edited *Fast Break to Line Break: Poets on the Art of Basketball* (Michigan State University Press, 2012) and co-edited *Making Poems: Forty Poems with Commentary by the Poets* (State University of New York Press, 2010). His poetry has appeared widely in such places as *American Poetry Review*, *Gettysburg Review*, *Shenandoah*, *North American Review*, and *Iowa Review*.

Claudia Emerson received the Pulitzer Prize for Poetry in 2006 for her collection, *Late Wife*. She has also been the recipient of fellowships from the NEA and the Guggenheim Foundation. She teaches at the University of Mary Washington in Virginia where in 2003 she was awarded the "Outstanding Young Faculty Award" for her teaching by the Alumni Foundation. She is the current Poet Laureate of Virginia.

Lisa Giles teaches creative writing, American poetry, environmental literature, and other courses at the University of Southern Maine and the University of New England. Her poems have been published in *Hayden's Ferry Review*, *Black Fly Review*, *California Quarterly*, *Hawaii Pacific Review*, and *Spoon River Poetry Review*. She holds an MFA in poetry from Arizona State and a PhD in American Literature at Brandeis University. She recently attended the Provost's Writing Seminar for USM Faculty and has been praised for fostering active learning in her students. Supporting the literary arts in her native state of Maine, she serves as a judge in the Poetry Out Loud program for local high school students.

Megan Grumbling teaches developmental writing at the University of New England and literature and creative writing at Southern Maine Community College. She has also been a poetry mentor to a city police officer, visited with women inmates as a guest poet, and led a nature writing workshop with practicing Buddhists. Her work has appeared in *Poetry, The Iowa Review, Crazyhorse, The Antioch Review*, and other journals, and was awarded a Ruth Lilly Poetry Fellowship and a Robert Frost Award. She serves as reviews editor for *The Cafe Review*, an arts and poetry journal based in Portland, and is the theater critic of *The Portland Phoenix*.

Bruce Guernsey is Distinguished Professor Emeritus at Eastern Illinois University where he taught 19th Century American Literature and Creative Writing for twenty-five years. He has also taught at William and Mary, Johns Hopkins, and Virginia Wesleyan where he was Poet in Residence for four years. He was awarded seven faculty excellence awards for teaching at Eastern Illinois, and in 1992-93, was selected as the State of Illinois Board of

Governors' "Professor of the Year," the highest award
in that state system. He has also been the recipient of
two Senior Fulbright Lectureships in American Poetry
to Portugal and to Greece and has twice sailed around
the world as a faculty member with Semester at Sea. His
poems have appeared in *The Atlantic, Poetry, The American
Scholar,* and his most recent book is *FROM RAIN: Poems,
1970-2010* (Ecco Qua Press, 2012). He is a former editor of *The Spoon River Poetry Review.*

Ted Kooser was the United States Poet Laureate from
2004-2006 and was honored with the Pulitzer Prize in
Poetry for his collection, *Delights and Shadows* in 2005.
As Poet Laureate, he started and still edits *American Life
in Poetry,* a weekly column that is published in newspa-
pers and periodicals around the world. In their simple
language and familiar themes, each poem of the week
in *ALP* reminds its millions of readers of our common humanity, a lesson that makes Mr. Kooser one of
our finest teachers.

Laurie Lamon is a Professor of English at Whitworth
University in Spokane, Washington. Her poems have
appeared in journals such as *The Atlantic Monthly, The
New Republic, Ploughshares, Colorado Review,* and *Arts &
Letters Journal of Contemporary Culture* and is included in
180 More Extraordinary Poems for Ordinary Days, edited

by Billy Collins; her poetry collections are *The Fork Without Hunger*, CavanKerry Press, 2005 and *Without Wings*, 2009. She was selected by Donald Hall, Poet Laureate 2007, as a Witter Bynner Fellow for '07, and is the recipient of a Washington State Artist Trust Award in 2005, a Graves Award for excellence in teaching in 2002, and a Pushcart Prize in 2001.

Diane Lockward was a high school English teacher for 25 years and received three Superintendent's Achievement Awards as well as a commendation from Tufts University for Excellence in Teaching; she now works as a poet-in-the-schools. She is the author of three poetry books, most recently, *Temptation by Water*, and two chapbooks; her work has been featured on *Poetry Daily* and *Verse Daily* and read by Garrison Keillor on *The Writer's Almanac*. The recipient of a Poetry Fellowship from the New Jersey State Council on the Arts and the 2006 Quentin R. Howard Poetry Prize, she was a Guest Poet at The Frost Place Conference on Poetry and Teaching.

M. B. McLatchey's debut poetry collection, *The Lame God*, won the May Swenson Award and will be published by Utah State in the Fall of 2013. Her recognition for excellence in teaching includes Harvard University's Danforth Prize and Brown University's Elmer Smith

Award. She holds a Masters degree in Comparative Literature from Harvard, the Masters in Teaching from Brown University, the M.F.A. from Goddard College, and a B.A. from Williams College. Over the past twenty years, she has directed writing workshops and she has taught literature and writing at Harvard, Rollins College, Valencia Community College, and the University of Central Florida. Currently, she is Assistant Professor of Writing and Humanities at Embry-Riddle Aeronautical University.

Wesley McNair is the author of nine collections of poetry and several of prose. His awards for poetry include two fellowships each from the NEA and the Rockefeller Foundations, as well as a Guggenheim Fellowship. The founder and director of the creative writing program at the University of Maine at Farmington, where he received the Distinguished Faculty Award, he has taught poetry writing throughout his career as an educator, serving also as a visiting professor in creative writing at Dartmouth and Colby Colleges. McNair has offered several workshops in poetry for high-school teachers in both Maine and New Hampshire, invited by state branches of the NEH. Retired since 2004, McNair is now Writer in Residence at UMF. In 2011, he was appointed as Maine's Poet Laureate.

Miho Nonaka is a native of Tokyo and a bilingual poet who has taught English and Creative Writing courses at Eastern Illinois University and Wheaton College. Her poetry and nonfiction have appeared or are forthcoming in *The Iowa Review*, *Ploughshares*, *Tin House*, *Cimarron Review*, *American Letters & Commentary*, among others. She received a Pushcart Prize nomination for poetry in 2007, and her work was chosen by Mark Doty to be included in *Helen Burns Poetry Anthology: New Voices from the Academy of American Poets' University & College Prizes, 1999-2008.*

Charlotte Pence is the author of two award-winning poetry chapbooks and the editor of *The Poetics of American Song Lyrics*, an essay collection on the similarities and differences between poetry and songs. Her first full-length poetry collection, *Spike*, is due out in 2014 by Black Lawrence Press. She also is the author of *The Writer's Path: Creative Exercises for Meaningful Essays,* which applies creative writing techniques to composition essays, an approach she has honed from fifteen years of teaching. She is married to the fiction writer Adam Prince and will join the creative writing faculty at Eastern Illinois University in 2013.

Sheryl St. Germain has been teaching at the university level for twenty-seven years and is currently

Director of the MFA Program in Creative Writing at Chatham University in Pittsburgh. Her work has won NEH and NEA awards as well as, most recently, the William Faulkner award for the personal essay. She has published four books of poetry, the most recent of which is *Let it Be a Dark Roux: New and Selected Poems;* a book of lyric essays, *Swamp Songs: the Making of an Unruly Woman*; and has co-edited a collection of essays, *Between Song and Story: Essays for the21st Century.* Her book of essays, *Navigating Disaster: Sixteen Songs of Love and a Poem of Despair* was published in Summer 2012.

Betsy Sholl's teaching experience ranges from work in prisons to creative writing classes at MIT; she has been teaching at the University of Southern Maine since 1983, and since 1993 in the Vermont College Masters of Fine Arts program, where she twice won the Crowley/Weingarten Award for Excellence in Teaching. She has published seven collections of poetry and among her awards are the Associated Writing Programs Prize for Poetry and the Felix Pollak Prize; from 2006 to 2011 she was Poet Laureate of Maine. She has received grants from the National Endowment for the Arts and the Maine Arts Commission.

Kevin Stein's thirty-six year teaching record includes stints as graduate student as well as Caterpillar Professor of English at Bradley University. At Bradley, he was named Faculty Member of the Year in recognition of outstanding classroom instruction. He publications include the forthcoming collection *Wrestling Li Po for the Remote* (Fifth Star Press) and ten other books of poetry, criticism, and anthology. Among his recent books are the essays of *Poetry's Afterlife: Verse in the Digital Age* (University of Michigan Press, 2010) and the verse collection *American Ghost Roses* (University of Illinois, 2005), winner of the Society of Midland Authors Poetry Award. His poems have earned the Frederick Bock Prize from *Poetry*, the *Indiana Review Poetry Prize*, the *Devins Award*, an NEA fellowship, and other distinctions. Since 2003 he's served as Illinois Poet Laureate.

Doug Sutton-Ramspeck has taught at The Ohio State University at Lima since 1999, and in that time he has been selected four times by students for the President's Salute, which honors teachers who, according to students, have had the most important influence on their academic lives. Only a few dozen professors are selected each year for this award from the many campuses of the Ohio State University system. In addition, Sutton-Ramspeck, author of four collections of poetry--including the John Ciardi and Barrow Street Press prize-winning books--has sponsored for the past ten years the Buckeye Creativity Awards for Allen County High School Students, which has honored more than 200 students and published more than 500 in the online literary journal *Hog Creek Review.*

Cecilia Woloch is the author of five collections of poems, most recently *Carpathia* (BOA Editions, 2009). The recipient of a 2011 National Endowment for the Arts fellowship, she teaches creative writing at the University of Southern California and has also conducted poetry workshops for thousands of children and young people throughout the United States and around the world, as well as workshops for senior citizens, inmates at a prison for the criminally insane, and residents at a shelter for homeless women. She spends part of each year traveling and in recent years has divided her time between Los Angeles; Atlanta; Shepherdsville, Kentucky; Paris, France; and a small village in the Carpathian mountains of southeastern Poland.

Baron Wormser is the co-author of the Heinemann book *A Surge of Language: Teaching Poetry Day by Day* now in its third printing and also is the co-author of *Teaching the Art of Poetry: the Moves* published in 2000 by Lawrence Erlbaum and still in print and part of the collection of many hundreds of libraries. Wormser has given workshops for the National Endowment for the Humanities, the NCTE and dozens of schools and school districts throughout the United States. Since 2000 he has directed the Conference on Poetry and Teaching at the Frost Place in Franconia, NH, where teachers gather each year to discuss the teaching of poetry.

Robert Wrigley is the author of eight books of poems, including, most recently, *Beautiful Country* (Penguin, 2010) and *Earthly Meditations: New and Selected Poems* (Penguin, 2006). Two new books will appear in the spring of 2013: The *Church of Omnivorous Light: Selected Poems* (Bloodaxe Books, in the UK); and *Anatomy of Melancholy* (Penguin). A former Guggenheim and two-time NEA Fellow, he teaches in the graduate writing program at the University of Idaho. He lives in the woods near Moscow, ID with his wife, the writer Kim Barnes.

SUBJECT INDEX

(Note: all the essays touch on the following topics, but those listed here tend to emphasize them)

Penyeach Press
is an independent publisher
that values precision in language
and clarity of vision.

Contact us at: penyeachpress@gmail.com

Made in the USA
Charleston, SC
02 March 2013